Learning Magento 2 Administration

Maximize the power of Magento 2 to improve your e-commerce business

Bret Williams

Cyndi Williams

BIRMINGHAM - MUMBAI

Learning Magento 2 Administration

First published: May 2016

Production reference: 1270516

Published by Packt Publishing Ltd.
Livery Place
35 Livery Street
Birmingham
B3 2PB, UK.
ISBN 978-1-78328-825-0

www.packtpub.com

Credits

Authors

Bret Williams

Cyndi Williams

Reviewer

Mathieu Nayrolles

Commissioning Editor

Vinay Argekar

Acquisition Editor

Vinay Argekar

Content Development Editor

Rashmi Suvarna

Technical Editor

Kunal Chaudhari

Copy Editors

Sonia Mathur

Shruti Iyer

Project Coordinator

Judie Jose

Proofreader

Safis Editing

Indexer

Mariammal Chettiyar

Graphics

Jason Monteiro

Production Coordinator

Melwyn Dsa

About the Authors

Bret Williams, for over 20 years, has engineered the creation of hundreds of websites, including many profitable e-commerce properties, as well as several Internet "firsts." Beginning with version 1.3 of Magento CE, Bret began an odyssey of becoming one of the foremost experts on leveraging Magento to build successful online businesses. Today, as CEO of novusweb llc, Bret continues to provide e-commerce management services from his office in Austin, Texas. Bret authored the wildly popular *Mastering Magento* and is co-author of the *Mastering Magento 2 Second Edition*, both Packt Publishing titles. His company also owns MageDaily.com, a Magento news and reviews blog, and MageRevolution.com, selling Magento enhancements.

Cyndi Williams has worked alongside Bret Williams—her husband of 35 years—building and managing e-commerce solutions, including their own successful online business, which they established in 2005, and later sold in 2009. As President of novusweb, llc, which is based in Austin, Texas, Cyndi focuses on managing online operations for select clients. Cyndi is an expert in operating Magento-based stores, as well as fulfillment, advertising, and social media management.

About the Reviewer

Mathieu Nayrolles was born in France and lived in a small village in *Côte d'Azur* for almost 15 years. He started his computer sciences studies in France and continued them in Montréal, Canada, where he now lives with his wife. Mathieu holds two master degrees from eXia.CESI in software engineering and UQAM in computer science. He is now a Ph.D student at Concordia University studying electrical and computer engineering, Montréal, Canada, under the supervision of Dr. Wahab Hamou-Lhadj.

During his academic journey, Mathieu has also worked for worldwide companies, such as Eurocopter and Saint-Gobain, where he learned how important good technical resources are.

You can discover some of his works through his books, *Xamarin Studio for Android Programming: A C# Cookbook, Mastering Apache Solr: A practical guide to get to grips with Apache Solr, Instant Magento Performances, Magento Performance Optimization: How to* and *Mastering Apache*, his blog (https://math.co.de/), or its latest realizations bumper-app.com, mindup.io, and toolwatch.io.

Follow @MathieuNls on twitter for even more information.

www.PacktPub.com

For support files and downloads related to your book, please visit www.PacktPub.com.

Did you know that Packt offers eBook versions of every book published, with PDF and ePub files available? You can upgrade to the eBook version at www.PacktPub.com and as a print book customer, you are entitled to a discount on the eBook copy. Get in touch with us at customercare@packtpub.com for more details.

At www.PacktPub.com, you can also read a collection of free technical articles, sign up for a range of free newsletters and receive exclusive discounts and offers on Packt books and eBooks.

https://www2.packtpub.com/books/subscription/packtlib

Do you need instant solutions to your IT questions? PacktLib is Packt's online digital book library. Here, you can search, access, and read Packt's entire library of books.

Why subscribe?

- Fully searchable across every book published by Packt
- Copy and paste, print, and bookmark content
- On demand and accessible via a web browser

Table of Contents

Preface

The release of Magento 2 marks a major milestone for the world's most successful open source e-commerce platform. This new version was completely rewritten, retooled, and redesigned to allow its merchants to move forward into the modern age of online commerce.

With this new version, many store owners will be joining the ranks of others who embrace the power and flexibility of Magento. However, like these Magento veterans, new owners will find Magento a bit intimidating at first. To be powerful, a platform must seem complex at times. To be sure, any top-end e-commerce system requires a depth of configurations, tools, and processes to truly be useful for merchants.

If you're familiar with Magento 1.x, you'll be happy to find much about Magento has also remained the same. At the same time, the core functionality that made Magento 1.x so very popular is now wrapped in a new and friendlier user interface. Workflows are improved and, as to be expected, much of the original functionality has evolved to be better than before!

In our work managing e-commerce stores and helping Magento store owners maximize profitability, we know that managing a Magento store can take a long time to master. We wanted to change this by condensing years of real world experience into a concise, easy-to-use manual that is specifically aimed at the Magento store operator.

Learning Magento 2 Administration is meant to be both a course of learning as well as a handy, daily reference book. In this book, our focus is on those who will be configuring and using Magento on a day-to-day basis. There are other great Packt Publishing books that dive deep into the technical development opportunities of Magento. Our book answers the question, "now what?" Once you have an installed Magento store, what can you do to give your store a competitive advantage? To leverage all the features of Magento? To operate your store efficiently?

We hope you find this "labor of love" as useful to you as it has been enjoyable for us to write. We also suspect you'll find many nuggets within these pages that make it a valuable asset for your Magento-related endeavors.

Regardless of where you are in using Magento 2 — considering, planning, launching, or operating — we suggest that you start by reading through this book in order. Learn where everything is and watch, especially, for the Tips sprinkled throughout. Then, use the book as a basis for creating your own action plans for improving your use of Magento.

Above all, enjoy using Magento 2. Embrace it and you'll prosper. You'll soon join the ranks of successful Magento-powered online stores.

What this book covers

Chapter 1, *Introducing Magento 2*, gives you a basic overview of the capabilities of Magento, what's new in Magento 2, and what's required for success with Magento.

Chapter 2, *Settings and Configurations*, is a menu-by-menu, screen-by-screen explanation of the Magento 2 backend configurations.

Chapter 3, *Catalogs and Stores*, give you an in-depth explanation of the powerful multistore feature of Magento and how to create manage multiple websites and languages.

Chapter 4, *Preparing to Sell,* discusses payments, shipping and taxes, and techniques and configurations to handle the "money" aspects of operating a Magento store.

Chapter 5, *Products,* contains explanations and guides to create and leverage different product types and tools.

Chapter 6, *Themes,* contains insights to choose and configure themes that give a Magento store a branded look and feel.

Chapter 7, *Content & SEO*, discusses specific instructions to manage nonproduct information and how to optimize information for search engines.

Chapter 8, *Promotions and Communication*, provides the reader with detailed guides to create promotional discounts, coupons, and newsletters to increase customer visits and engagement.

Chapter 9, *Security and Administration*, has key configurations to ensure that your Magento store is secure and optimized for speed and usability.

Chapter 10, *Startup Checklist*, this chapter is a step-by-step guide to prepare your new Magento 2 store for a successful launch.

What you need for this book

This book was written on the premise that you have — or will have — a working installation of Magento 2. The only tool that you'll need is your web browser to access your new site, both on the frontend and the backend.

Who this book is for

While developers should certainly learn the contents of this book in order to provide better counsel to their clients, this book is primarily aimed at the Magento 2 *Store Owner*. The day-to-day use of Magento as an e-commerce platform requires a deep understanding of many concepts and functions, some of which are unique to Magento.

Conventions

In this book, you will find a number of text styles that distinguish between different kinds of information. Here are some examples of these styles and an explanation of their meaning.

Code words in text, database table names, folder names, filenames, file extensions, pathnames, dummy URLs, user input, and Twitter handles are shown as follows: "you could view the category in your store by going to `yourstore.com/sofas.html` in your browser."

New terms and important words are shown in bold. Words that you see on the screen, for example, in menus or dialog boxes, appear in the text like this: "Click on the **Main Website Store** link in the Stores panel"

Warnings or important notes appear in a box like this.

Tips and tricks appear like this.

Reader feedback

Feedback from our readers is always welcome. Let us know what you think about this book-what you liked or disliked. Reader feedback is important for us as it helps us develop titles that you will really get the most out of.

To send us general feedback, simply e-mail feedback@packtpub.com, and mention the book's title in the subject of your message.

If there is a topic that you have expertise in and you are interested in either writing or contributing to a book, see our author guide at www.packtpub.com/authors .

Customer support

Now that you are the proud owner of a Packt book, we have a number of things to help you to get the most from your purchase.

Downloading the color images of this book

We also provide you with a PDF file that has color images of the screenshots/diagrams used in this book. The color images will help you better understand the changes in the output. You can download this file from `https://www.packtpub.com/sites/default/files/downloads/LearningMagento2Administration_ColorImages`.

Errata

Although we have taken every care to ensure the accuracy of our content, mistakes do happen. If you find a mistake in one of our books-maybe a mistake in the text or the code-we would be grateful if you could report this to us. By doing so, you can save other readers from frustration and help us improve subsequent versions of this book. If you find any errata, please report them by visiting `http://www.packtpub.com/submit-errata`, selecting your book, clicking on the **Errata Submission Form** link, and entering the details of your errata. Once your errata are verified, your submission will be accepted and the errata will be uploaded to our website or added to any list of existing errata under the Errata section of that title.

To view the previously submitted errata, go to `https://www.packtpub.com/books/content/support` and enter the name of the book in the search field. The required information will appear under the **Errata** section.

Piracy

Piracy of copyrighted material on the Internet is an ongoing problem across all media. At Packt, we take the protection of our copyright and licenses very seriously. If you come across any illegal copies of our works in any form on the Internet, please provide us with the location address or website name immediately so that we can pursue a remedy.

Please contact us at `copyright@packtpub.com` with a link to the suspected pirated material.

We appreciate your help in protecting our authors and our ability to bring you valuable content.

Questions

If you have a problem with any aspect of this book, you can contact us at `questions@packtpub.com`, and we will do our best to address the problem.

1
Introducing Magento 2

It's no secret that Magento is the world's leading open source e-commerce platform. According to *BuiltWith* website, since its introduction in 2008, the versatility and power of this system has helped it grow into an installed base of over 220,000 online stores. Thousands of developers work with store owners like you to harness this power to accommodate a wide variety of products, markets, and customer types. The "Magento ecosystem" includes thousands of third-party add-ons, design themes, and services that increase Magento's ability to fulfill almost any online commerce need.

However, as we all know, you can't stand still in the competitive world of e-commerce. Changes in the marketplace constantly force all of us to re-evaluate every aspect of our online efforts. Whether it's a change in Google's search algorithm, the impact of mobile commerce, or the ongoing influence of social media, those who stand still quickly fall behind.

The same goes for e-commerce technology. Despite changes in ownership over the past 3 years, Magento management has continued to push their teams to create the next, improved version of Magento. As we in the Magento community championed for some time, Magento needed more than incremental changes if it were to remain at the top of the charts. Magento needed a complete review and reworking of all its systems.

Today, we can now celebrate the completion of this huge undertaking. Magento 2 represents a total overhaul, poising it for the demands of e-commerce today and in the foreseeable future.

In this chapter, we'll cover:

- What's new in Magento 2
- Using Magento for e-commerce
- What you need to succeed with Magento

First, let's discuss for whom this book is primarily written.

A store owner's primer

This book is crafted to be an ideal companion for Magento store owners as they explore and benefit from the features and power of Magento 2. After installing and initially configuring a new Magento 2 store, what comes next? Once you read through this book, you'll be able to not only understand the various tools at your command, but you'll also be able to profit from operating a Magento-powered online store by leveraging these tools to your advantage.

You should also make a copy of this book available to others in your organization who:

- Process orders (refer to Chapter 3, *Catalogs & Stores*)
- Manage products (Chapter 4, *Preparing to Sell*)
- Handle design changes (Chapter 5, *Products*)
- Add and edit site content (Chapter 6, *Themes*)
- Promote your products and site (Chapter 7, *Content & SEO*)
- Are in charge of site security and technical issues (Chapter 8, *Promotions & Communication*)

Once you read through *Learning Magento 2 Administration*, you'll find a great checklist in Chapter 9, *Security and Administration* to make sure you address all the key configurations and processes when launching a new store.

What's new in Magento 2

If you currently use or have previously used a Magento 1.x store, you'll notice that many things look different in Magento 2. Throughout this book, you'll note from various screenshots that the backend interface is easier to use and rich in new operations features. We'll explore these in later chapters.

While the new UI is pretty slick, it's the under-the-hood improvements that you'll come to truly appreciate in your Magento store. Magento has long been challenged by a lack of speed. Even on servers and systems specifically tuned for Magento, heavy traffic from online visitors, large backend operations (for example, importing, reports, and so on), and inherent code bottlenecks have made many Magento stores slower performers than similar stores on other platforms. At times, it's even made us step back and compare the benefits of Magento against other platforms, although we keep coming back to Magento due to its unique features.

The Magento team focused considerable energy in making Magento faster. At the expense of getting too "geeky", let's explore some of the most important improvements:

- To improve scalability (which is the ability to increase resources during heavier traffic loads), Magento now includes *full page caching* as part of Community Edition. Caching reduces the number of operations needed to render a web page to your visitor, greatly improving user experience.

- The "rearchitecture" of the entire system has truly improved code efficiency. This work also helps developers by making the code simpler and more accessible.
- Magento 2 uses the latest **HTML 5** and **CSS 3** code frameworks optimized for modern browsers. In addition, CSS code can be more efficiently built in **SASS** and "preprocessed" by Magento. For theme designers, these features help create more mobile-ready designs that give your visitors a much richer shopping experience.
- Upgrades and add-ons are easier to use and manage. Magento is creating an extension verification program as well to validate new add-ons. There will be no more buying of third-party add-ons that break a Magento store due to poor coding.

Using Magento for e-commerce

People often ask us why we recommend Magento as an e-commerce platform more times than any other platform. After all, there are so many solutions available, many with less startup costs (and many with higher startup costs too).

The key to our recommendation is that as owners of e-commerce businesses ourselves, we know that operating a profitable and vibrant online store is much more complex than many would guess. If you've been in e-commerce already, you know too well that establishing, growing, and managing a web-based retail business can be every bit as challenging as building a brick-and-mortar business. Although the downside is much less than a traditional storefront, e-commerce adds business considerations and processes that are unique to online commerce, especially in today's highly competitive online marketplace.

If you haven't already, let's discuss some of the primary considerations of running an e-commerce business you do or will do and how Magento can help resolve them.

Selling complex products

It would make e-commerce so much easier if all products were alike—if we only sold shoes or backpacks online. Of course, this would make for a very small group of online stores.

Apparel, for instance, is one of the most complex products to sell online from a configuration and presentation aspect. Sizes, colors, collar styles, gender, and so on—so many *attributes* for each product. Add to this the idea that inventory for each *variant* may need to be tracked, and you can quickly see the challenges any platform has in providing customers with easy-to-use selections while meeting back-office business needs.

You may want to sell *bundles* of products, such as a bed linen collection with sheets, pillowcases, and duvets, yet also offer these products separately. This complexity can truly exceed the capability of many platforms.

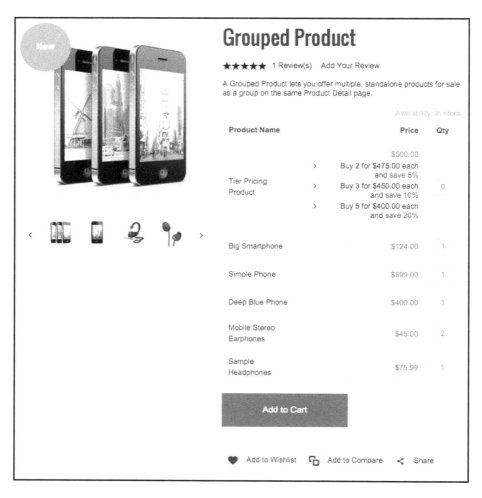

We work with clients who have tens of thousands of different products and others with many complex product types, such as variants and bundles. Magento's unique and extremely powerful management of attributes and product types is one of the most powerful reasons as to why we prefer Magento as a platform. We have yet to experience another platform that gives the store owner the depth and power to manage products from tractor parts to cleaning products and t-shirts to computers.

Managing multiple online stores

Many online businesses begin as sole stores selling a particular line of products or services. However, the relatively low cost of entry allows many merchants to develop multiple product lines or retail brands that can be managed by the same staff and resources.

Without having to install and manage multiple platforms, a company can manage all the products, customers, and web content with a single login. Although not generally a good idea due to logistical considerations, we've seen as many as 96 separate websites managed in a single Magento instance.

The multistore feature of Magento also allows the easy creation of multiple language versions of the same brand. Many global brands use Magento in order to provide content in multiple languages.

It was the multiple store feature of Magento that originally lead us to commit our own resources to learning Magento several years ago, and it continues to feed our interest in this evolving platform today.

Extending functionality

We have yet to work with a client that doesn't need to add some feature or function to the base Magento installation, not because Magento is weak but rather because Magento is so capable of supporting the myriad of business needs across so many retail and wholesale sectors.

Many popular hosted solutions, such as Shopify and BigCommerce, are subject to limitations in functionality because their code base is "locked down." In other words, if you want additional features added to these platforms, you're limited to only what these platforms expose via their **Application Programming Interface** (**API**). While there are many add-ons available to these platforms, customization is still limited.

Magento is an Open Source platform. This means that the code is fully exposed and can be customized however needed. We've worked with a client who wanted to present their products in a unique manner that was not natively supported in Magento, and there was no third-party extension to meet their needs. We were able to easily add code to the Magento code that solved their requirement. This particular modification would not have been possible with a closed platform.

In addition to the customization of the Magento code, more features can be added using third-party extensions. With Magento 1.x, there were over 3,000 extensions offered on Magento Connect (`www.magentocommerce.com/magento-connect`). Hundreds more are available via other outlets such as Code Canyon (www.codecanyon.net). This is, by far, the largest collection of add-ons for any popular platform.

Global e-commerce

Of all the popular platforms we continue to review and analyze, Magento remains the leader in providing true global e-commerce capabilities. From the built-in currency conversion updater to the inline language translation feature, Magento is built for global commerce.

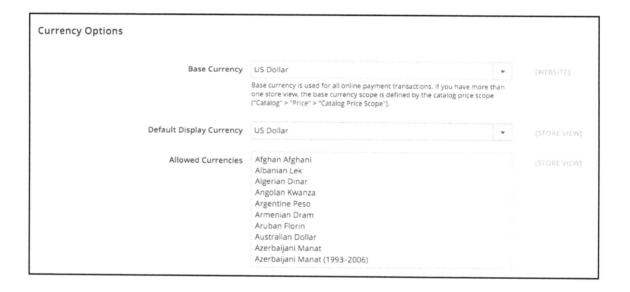

What you need to succeed with Magento

Some might answer "courage." In fact, after writing *Mastering Magento* (also from Packt Publishing), we heard from a lot of readers how they struggled with Magento and how undertrained developers jeopardized their Magento stores with poor coding. Many store owners have less than stellar experiences with Magento, and as a result, Magento has earned a dubious reputation on many blogs and forums.

We would suggest that a better requirement for success is "planning." In fact, planning is the focus of Chapter 9, *Security and Administration* of this book. If you understand how Magento works and take the time to construct a proper plan to fulfill the requirements of this incredible platform, you'll have much better success.

As a store owner, though, don't expect to install, configure, and design a Magento store by yourself. Unless you have real experience with Magento, it's best to find a professional with strong Magento skills. And, hopefully, you find one that understands e-commerce and not just the programming aspects. The right partnership will ultimately save you thousands of dollars in lost opportunity as well as direct costs. If you already have Magento 2 installed, we suggest giving a copy of this book to your developer, as well, so that both of you are on the same page. The more they know about how you wish to run your business, the better they can help make sure that Magento is configured "under the hood" for your purposes.

Summary

If you're building a store in Magento, you're embarking on a wonderfully exciting journey into serious e-commerce. You may be moving from a less powerful platform or migrating from an earlier version of Magento. However you arrived to this point, you'll be using the most advanced open source platform in the world. The power of Magento also gives this platform considerable complexity. This book is created to help you navigate the operational aspects of your Magento store and give you the confidence to build a successful and profitable online business. Magento 2 is more powerful, runs faster, and has more features than Magento 1.x. With this book in hand, you're ready to take full advantage of Magento 2.

In the next chapter, we'll begin this journey from the topmost level: your stores and catalogs.

2

Settings and Configurations

If you've ever used Magento in the past to operate an online store, you'll find that the backend of Magento 2 has changed considerably. The developers at Magento basically started from scratch in redesigning the administrative portal.

The **user interface** (**UI**) of the backend is much cleaner, more readable, and more logical. It was created on top of a *responsive* framework so that you can manage your store using anything from a tablet to a desktop computer, and the UI adjusts accordingly. The backend still won't work on a smartphone, as managing a Magento store on a phone would be incredibly difficult. The UI designers also improved grids—the table—style listing of products, customers, and so on—which makes it much easier to get your work done.

But more than just a pretty face, the Magento backend is your store's "back office." It is the place where you control how your store will operate, as well as what it will sell. Any retail business has certain business rules, such as shipping, payments, inventory management, returns and refunds, currency conversions, and much more.

Once you understand the many configurations possible in a Magento 2 installation, you'll realize your desired processes better, and will be able to leverage Magento to increase sales, satisfy more customers, and improve your e-commerce profitability.

In this chapter, we will do the following things:

- Introduce you to the Magento 2 backend
- Explain key system settings

Introducing the Magento 2 backend

The new UI of Magento 2 is quite a change from the original Magento admin backend. Whereas Magento 1.x had a more traditional layout, Magento 2 leverages the best of HTML 5 and CSS 3 to create a responsive interface, which we're sure you'll find more enjoyable.

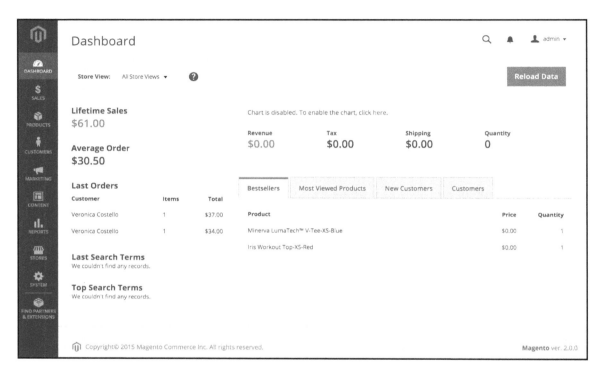

The primary navigation menu is located along the left side of the window. This placement gives more space to the content of whatever section you're working in. Each of the main menu items has a pop-out menu of choices within that group.

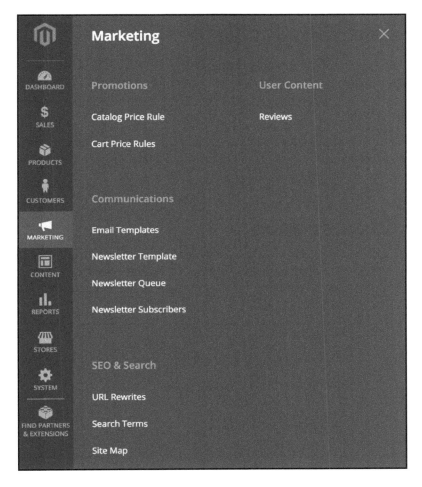

In the upper-right corner of the backend, there are three icons: search, notifications, and account:

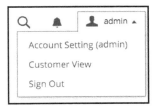

Global search allows you to search for anything in the backend: products, customers, orders, and so on. It's a wonderful way to quickly search for whatever you need without having to first drill down through several menu levels.

The bell icon takes you to a list of notifications, if any. If a "badge" (a red circle with a number) appears, it means you have received notifications from Magento or extension developers alerting you to updates or other important information. Click this icon to view and process notifications.

The account drop-down menu gives you access to your **Account Settings**, where you can update your name and password. By clicking on **Customer View**, a new tab will open to display the frontend of your Magento store.

Configuration scopes

In Chapter 3, *Catalogs and Stores*, we'll go into more depth regarding multiple websites, stores, and store views. However, as we are going to discuss configurations now, it's important that we take a moment to explain the section following the title of the screen.

The **Store View** menu allows you to set the *configuration scope* for whatever you wish to do in the backend. Depending on the screen you're viewing, you can switch between **All Store Views**, a particular website, or store view within your Magento installation.

This is a very important concept, as your actions can impact everything in your store, a website, or store view. Likewise for reviewing information: you can view information for all the stores in your installation, or those of a single store.

As you work through the Magento backend, be sure to be aware of your configuration scope setting. Some configurations can be set at the Website and/or Store View level as well, giving you an incredible flexibility to have different configurations for different stores. See `Chapter 3`, *Catalogs and Stores*, to learn more about multiple stores.

Besides many configurations, you may see **[GLOBAL]**, **[WEBSITE]**, or **[STORE VIEW]**. This indicates the finest level at which this configuration can be set. In other words, if you see **[WEBSITE]** beside a configuration, you could set a different value if your configuration scope is set at a particular website within your configuration. A **[STORE VIEW]** label means you can set values particular to a Store View level.

When you are at any configuration scope other than the Global (or Default) level, you will see a checkbox selector:

With the box checked, the setting shown will be *inherited* from the higher scope level. In the preceding image—captured at a Store View configuration scope—the selected checkbox means that the associated setting will be the same as that of the Website configuration scope. If you uncheck this box, you can set a different value for the particular Store View configuration scope in which you're working.

 Not all configuration settings are possible at all configuration scope levels. For example, the activation of a payment method (like Credit Card, PayPal, and so on) can only be set at the Website level, not at the Store View configuration scope level. If you're at a level in which a setting is not applicable, it will not appear. So, don't be alarmed if certain settings "disappear" as you change from one scope level to another.

As we go through the many configurations within Magento, we will be reviewing them at the Global level so we can discuss all possible choices. Note the configuration scope level shown to the right of each configuration to understand the maximum depth at which you can fine-tune your store or stores.

Key system configurations

Magento's real power comes from its ability to adapt and accommodate almost any type of online selling needs. We will go through the most important backend configurations that you need to review when setting up a new Magento store. As you'll see, there are many settings. However, the more you know about how they affect your store, the more productive your selling opportunities can be.

The various configurations we are going to discuss are contained within two main navigation menus: **Stores** and **System**. First, let's explore the **Stores** menu.

 For now, we will approach configurations as if you have a single Magento store front. Setting up and configuring multiple stores in a single installation will be covered in Chapter 3, *Catalogs and Stores*.

Configuration

There are six side tabs under the **Stores** top-level menu on the **Configuration** screen: **General**, **Catalog**, **Customers**, **Sales**, **Services**, and **Advanced**. Let's discuss each configuration set.

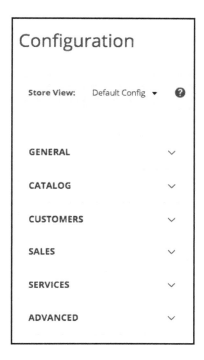

To expand each side menu, click on the down arrow on the right, and click to select a sub-menu item. The main content area of your screen will then contain various *configuration panels*. To expand each panel, click the down arrow within a circle located to the far right of each panel title.

General panels

Under the General panel you would see the following options:

General settings

You will find the following options within the **General** settings of the **General** panel (yes, we know it's a bit confusing):

Country Options

- **Default Country**: Select the "home" country for the store. If you're building multiple stores, you can select a different **Default Country** for each store.
- **Allow Countries**: Set the countries from where you will allow certain activities within your site. As you go through various settings for payments, shipping, and more, you will have the option to allow certain activities with Allowed Countries or to select certain target countries. If you know you're only going to do business within a select group of countries, you can preselect that group within this configuration.

- **Zip/Postal Code is Optional for**: You can also add to the countries for which a postal code is optional (not required, but desired).
- **European Union Countries**: Change the selection of countries that are part of the European Union (this does change from time to time).
- **Top Destinations**: The countries you select in this list will appear at the top of any country selection list. For instance, if you select **United Kingdom** and **United States**, the Country selector on the Checkout page would list these countries at the top and all other Allowed Countries in the list below.

When configuring multi-select fields (such as the list of Allowed Countries), scroll through the list to see what is already selected by default. If you wish to add to those selected, click while holding the *Ctrl* key (*cmd* for Macs). Likewise, use this to de-select the selected values. In this way, you don't change other already-selected values. If you make a selection error, simply refresh your web page and try again.

State Options

- **State is Required for**: Add or subtract from the list of countries in which the selection of a state is required during checkout or account registration. The United States is one, for example, in which you will want to require a state selection.

- **Allow to Choose State if It is Optional for Country**: In some cases, the selection of a state or province is not required, yet you may want the user to have the ability to enter one.

Locale Options

- **Timezone**: Set the applicable time zone for your store.
- **Locale**: This sets the regional language and formats for your store. For instance, if you choose **English (United States)**, the store language will be English and numbers will appear as 9,999.00.
- **Weight Unit**: Choose pounds (**lbs**) or kilograms (**kgs**) as the default weight measure.
- **First Day of Week**: Many countries consider Monday as the first day of the Week. In the USA, Sunday is generally considered the first day of the week. This setting affects reports showing weekly activity (for example, sales).
- **Weekend Days**: If you want to separate the weekends from weekdays, select the days that are considered weekend days.

Store Information

The information here will be available to shoppers, and should reflect the information you wish to communicate for your store (which may be different from your actual business entity).

Single-Store Mode

If you're sure you will not use multiple stores in your Magento installation, you can set **Enable Single-Store Mode** to **Yes**. This will remove the configuration scope choices, and prevent you from making different configurations at the Website and/or Store View levels. When selected (and saved), the Configuration Scope menu at the top-left of your screen will be removed, as will the scope labels beside each configuration field.

Even if you plan to possibly use multiple stores later on, enabling the single-store mode can, for now, avoid any confusion when configuring your stores. Unless you're intent on immediately configuring multiple Websites or Stores, we recommend using this feature to reduce backend complexity. Once you add additional Websites or Stores, this selection becomes moot.

When saving configurations, you may see a warning that you need to review your caching or indexing. We will discuss these important Magento features later in the chapter.

Web settings

The Web settings are settings that affect public access to your site.

Be very careful when changing the settings in this section, as they can easily disable your site. A qualified Magento developer can help advise you on these settings, as they can also be affected by how your site is installed and configured on a server. *If you don't understand a setting here, do not change it.*

URL Options

Consult your Magento developer for these settings. We select **add store codes to URLs** when we build a store that will use a common SSL URL (for example, `https://www.domain.com`) across multiple stores with different domains. Otherwise, this is probably not needed.

A **Uniform Resource Locator** (**URL**) is the full web address, such as `http://www.domain.com` or `https://www.domain.com`.

In most cases, you will want to select **Auto-redirect to Base URL**, as this will help prevent duplicate content. We usually set this to **Yes (301 Move Permanently)**.

Search Engine Optimization.

In most cases, you will want to use **Web Server Rewrites**.

Search Engine Optimization (**SEO**) is much, much more than just this setting, of course. In `Chapter 7`, *Content and SEO*, we will discuss ways to improve your search engine visibility.

Base URLs

The base URL is the web address that people will use to access your website. You can set different URLs for static view and media files in the event that you're using a different server for delivering these assets. Your developer can best advise you on these settings.

Base URLs (Secure)

Security for your customers (and for you) is very important. Once you have an SSL certificate installed on your server, you can enter the secure URL for your site here. You can also choose to secure the frontend of your site, as well as the admin backend.

 Google has started to reward websites that use SSL encryption throughout the site. Therefore, when you have SSL installed on your server, you should use secure URLs on your storefront.

Default Pages

Your site will contain pages of information, not just categories and products. In Chapter 7, *Content and SEO*, we will discuss content pages in more detail. In this section, you will create the pointers that allow Magento to respond to various requests for your Home page, the "404 Page Not Found" page, and a page to warn users that they need to have cookies enabled.

Breadcrumbs are the navigation items shown at the top of a page that show a user where they are in your site in relation to the Home page. For example Home > Contact Us tells the user that they are on the Contact Us page, which is one level down from the Home page (which is clickable).

Default Cookie Settings

Cookies are the small, invisible files created when you browse the web that allow websites to save information on your computer. This information helps websites keep track of your activities, such as your shopping cart, number of visits, and authorizations. For instance, as you work in the Magento backend, a cookie lets Magento know that you're an approved backend user. It also notes the last time you visited a page so that Magento, as a security measure, can request that you log in again if a certain amount of time has elapsed since your last visit. In this section, you can set the amount of time that a customer cookie is valid for (in seconds). If you want a customer's session to last longer than one hour (3,600 seconds), you can increase this amount. For sites that will be using Google analytics and/or selling to countries in Europe, you should activate the **Cookie Restriction Mode**. This gives the user a message that cookies will be used, and asks for their permission to allow it. Once allowed, the message will disappear.

 To edit the *Cookie Restriction Message*, go to **CMS | Static Blocks**, and find the **Cookie Restriction Notice**. For more on editing static blocks, see Chapter 7, *Content and SEO*.

Session Validation Settings

Do not change these settings without consulting your Magento developer.

Browser Capabilities Detection

If you want to properly handle users who have disabled cookies or JavaScript—both important for the operation of your store—you should leave these set to **Yes**.

Local Storage refers to a feature of HTML5 that enables storage of data locally on a user's computer rather than only in cookies. Local storage is more secure, and can hold more data. If you wish to provide a warning to users when their browser does not support local storage, select **Yes**.

Design settings

The Design settings address both the appearance of your store as well as certain "under the hood" code to improve your site's visibility.

Design Theme

In this panel, you can select any of the Magento themes properly installed on your server. If you have different themes installed for various browser or device types, you can specify them here (see your developer for specific information).

HTML Head

The "head" of your website is the code within each page that provides key information to your browser.

- **Favicon icon**: The small icon that appears in a browser tag or address line. You should prepare a square image of your logo or symbol. The minimum size should be 16×16 pixels, but a larger image can be used as long as it is square. For maximum compatibility across browsers, use an ICO or PNG format file.
- **Default Title**: This will appear as the **Page Title** of any page not otherwise specified (see more in `Chapter 7`, *Content and SEO*).
- **Title Prefix** and **Title Suffix**: These will be prepended or appended, respectively, to any Page Title. For example, if you want My Company to appear after any Page Title, enter it in the **Title Suffix** field.
- **Default Description** and **Default Keywords**: These are the text that will appear whenever you have not specified other values in products, categories, or pages.

- **Miscellaneous Scripts:** Any scripts that you need to add to the page head (such as tracking or pop-up scripts) can be added in this field.

> By default, Magento includes `<link rel="stylesheet" type="text/css" media="all" href="{{MEDIA_URL}}styles.css" />` in the **Miscellaneous Scripts** field. This is to pull in the CSS file applicable to your store, based on the media URL that you specified, if any, in the **Web** settings panel.

- **Display Demo Store Notice**: To give notice to visitors that your store is under development and will not honor orders, set to **Yes**.

> As we will discuss in `Chapter 7`, *Content and SEO*, good SEO is important for elevating your store in Google rankings. We suggest that you leave the **Default Description** and **Default Keywords** fields blank to avoid duplicate meta content, which could be adverse to your SEO efforts. Commit now to address the description field in every category, product, and CMS page and you'll have better results. The **Meta Keywords** field is virtually ignored by search engines, but, if used, should be attended to with the same dedication as your description field.

Search Engine Robots

When search engines visit your site, they first look to find the `robots.txt` file. This file gives instructions as to what the search engine should and should not index and display in their ranking listings. While you're building your store—particularly if it can be found by others on the Web—you should set **Default Robots** to **NOINDEX, NOFOLLOW**. This will prevent search engines from parsing your store until it's ready. Afterwards, set this to **INDEX, FOLLOW**.

- **Edit custom instructions of the robots.txt file**: For the first time, Magento now allows you to manage the contents of the `robots.txt` file. If you have other indexing conditions, you can add them to the `robots.txt` file. In `Chapter 7`, *Content and SEO* we will provide you with the default `robots.txt` file that we use in our Magento stores.

Header

- **Logo Image**: Upload a logo file that will usually appear at the top of your website (this depends on your design theme). You should upload a file that is no more than twice the size in which it will display.

One of the most common mistakes we see is the use of an image that is much larger than the space in which it is contained. For instance, if the area for your logo is 400×100 pixels, don't upload a 2000×500 pixel image. While it will be displayed in a smaller size, you'll be asking users to wait while their browser downloads a much larger file. This goes for photos and other images: don't tax your users' patience by using images that are larger than their final display size. The one exception is product photos. Magento will resize product images as needed, and the larger the original image, the better the final results—in most cases. Depending on your logo, you should try to use a PNG format file. It will retain details better than JPG files, particularly if the logo is a graphic rather than a photo. One exception to the size rule is the *retina displays*. New generation iPhones, iPads, and iMacs have high-resolution displays. To give your logo a better, sharper image for these devices, use an image that is exactly twice the size of the intended size. For example, if your logo display area is 400×100 pixels, upload a logo image of 800×200 pixels. Some themes may accommodate two logo images—one for normal and one for retina displays. Consult your theme information for more details.

- **Logo Image Width** and **Logo Image Height**: In these fields, you can specify the exact size of your logo image as you would like it to be displayed on your site. Some themes will restrict the size (usually height), so you may need to have your developer adjust your theme should you desire a larger logo size than what is allowed by the theme.

- **Logo Image Alt**: For SEO purposes, it's important that every image in your store has an Image Alt value. This is a hidden value that describes the image. For this field, you might enter `Acme Hardware Logo`. This tells search engines what the image is, since they can't discern the contents of an image.

- **Welcome Text**: Depending on the theme used, a welcome message can be displayed, usually at the top of the page:

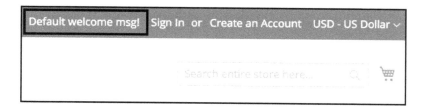

Footer

- **Copyright**: You may enter the text that you want to appear at the bottom of your web pages.
- **Miscellaneous HTML**: This field can be useful when you need to insert JavaScript code snippets for tracking or other features. While you can do this, as mentioned previously in the **Header** section, some services will request that you place the code at the end of your page code. This field places whatever you place inside as the last item before the ending `</body>` tag.

Product Image Watermarks

Watermarks are images that are overlaid on your product images. You may notice on some e-commerce sites that the store name is placed on the product image as semi-transparent text.

By adding a graphic with a transparent background, you can overlay your store name, URL, copyright, and so on.

Personally, we're not big fans of overlays that detract from the photo or product detail. We understand that some merchants are trying to battle plagiarism of their images, but we feel a better approach is to "brand" your imagery using themed backgrounds. In the image that follows, notice the branding "star" of the company's logo and the ©ADC in the lower-right corner. By using this theme throughout the site, American Dictation (`http://www.AmericanDication.com`) has built branding consistency while providing some difficulties for others who wish to repurpose their images as their own. Interestingly, we've found that most images which have intrusive overlays are actually images provided by manufacturers, and are not original photos owned by the merchant.

Recently, we had a client who told them that Google was disallowing their products for Google Shopping because their images had watermarks on them.

There are three image sizes for each product image (we'll cover this in detail in `Chapter 5`, *Products)*: Base, Small, and Thumbnail. You can set the watermark image for each size in this section, each with the same available settings described as follows:

- **Image Watermark Default Size**: Enter the size in pixels (width x height) of your overlay.
- **Image Watermark Opacity, Percent**: Enter the percentage (without %) of opacity, or transparency, that you want for your image. The lower the percentage, the more transparent your image.
- **Image Watermark**: Find and upload your watermark file.

The background of a JPEG image (`.jpg` and `.jpeg`) cannot be made transparent as with a GIF or PNG file. If you want to overlay text or a logo without the background of the image, save it as a GIF or PNG with transparency. JPEGs are better for images or photos you may wish to use as an overlay.

- **Image Watermark Position**: Set how you wish your watermark to be displayed on top of product images. **Stretch** will resize your watermark, both in width and height, to match that of the overlaid image. **Tile** will repeat your image, both horizontally and vertically, to fill the image area. Other selections will place a watermark image, in its default size, at a set position over the product image.

Pagination

New to Magento 2 is the ability to control the pagination that appears at the bottom of categories that have more products than can be displayed on a single page.

 In the **Catalog** Panels discussed later in this chapter, you can control the number of products to be displayed on a single page.

- **Pagination Frame**: Enter an integer value such as 1, 2, 3, 4, and so on for the most page links that you wish to display at the bottom of the page.
- **Pagination Frame Skip**: Let's say your category listing requires 20 pages of products. If you set your **Pagination Frame** to 5, then you would make it difficult for customers to reach the later pages without having to make a lot of clicks. It might be more user-friendly to have a link beyond page 5 that takes the user to page 10 so as to skip more rapidly through your list. The value in this field will add links to your pagination to allow skipping to further pages (when available).
- **Anchor Text for Previous/Anchor Text for Next**: If you don't want arrows at the beginning and end of your pagination frame, you can enter text that you wish to use, such as Prev and Next, or Anterior and Después (Spanish).

Transactional E-mails

In Chapter 8, *Promotions and Communication* we will talk more about the many e-mails that are generated by various events in Magento (for example, orders, new accounts, and so on). You can upload your store logo for use in these e-mails as well as include an image ALT text.

 While you may be able to style your logo's size when creating custom e-mail Templates (as discussed in Chapter 8, *Promotions & Communication*), you should probably limit your logo size to somewhere around 200-300 pixels wide and no more than 100 pixels tall so that it doesn't dominate the e-mail view, especially in mobile e-mail views.

New to Magento 2 is the ability to create header and footer templates that can be used on all e-mails. This makes it much easier to change information such as business hours or phone numbers across all e-mails.

Currency Setup settings

In today's global economy, it's not uncommon for online retailers to accommodate customers in many countries and areas of the world. While you don't have to offer your products in multiple currencies, you may wish to do so.

There are two approaches you can take to offering multiple currencies for your online business: **automated currency conversions** and **static currency pricing**. With automated conversions, as discussed later in Chapter 3, *Catalogs and Stores*, you will have a single Store View with a drop-down menu allowing customers to display prices in different *converted* currencies based on the current currency *conversion ratios*. Alternatively, you can create multiple Store Views, each with its own default currency (like US Dollar, British Pound Sterling, Euro, and so on), and enter a specific, *static* price for a product for each Store View. Some businesses prefer this method, as it allows you to adjust the price for specific currencies based on regional costs (you may be shipping UK products from a UK-based warehouse, and US products from a US-based warehouse, each with its own cost structure).

- **Base Currency**: Select the currency you wish to use for your payment transactions. You may want to use **US Dollars** for your payment gateway transactions (like PayPal, Stripe, and so on), but display your primary currency in another currency (next setting).
- **Default Display Currency**: As mentioned earlier, you can display your default currency in any desired currency.
- **Allowed Currencies**: If you select more than one currency in this field, Magento will display a drop-down currency selection menu on your site allowing customers to select from among the currencies selected.

There are additional settings and configurations required to present multiple currencies on your site. See Chapter 3, *Catalogs and Stores*, for more information on how to complete this process.

Webservicex

WebserviceX.NET is a free service that provides connectivity with a wide variety of online databases and services. Magento uses this to retrieve currency conversion factors for updating currency ratios (for example, US Dollars to Euros).

- **Connection Timeout in Seconds**: You should not need to alter this value, which is the amount of time Magento should wait for a response from WebserviceX.NET. If you get timeout messages e-mailed to you regularly (see next panel), you might consider increasing this number, as your web server may be experiencing delays in sending and receiving the currency update request.

Scheduled Import Settings

If you plan to use automated currency conversions, you'll need to enable the WebserviceX.NET service.

 There are some alternatives to WebserviceX.NET for prior versions of Magento, but we're unaware of any for Magento 2 at this point. Personally, we haven't found any reason to use another service, but if you find the conversion rates provided by WebserviceX.NET are not accurate for your purposes, you might scout for other alternatives.

- **Enabled**: Set to **Yes** to enable currency conversion updates.
- **Service**: At present, only **Webservicex** is available.
- **Start Time**: Enter the time according to the time zone of your installation server. You may want to update values after major markets close or at midnight (default setting).
- **Frequency**: Select how often you want to update currency ratios.
- **Error Email Recipient**: You'll see this in several places throughout the configuration panels. This allows you to enter an e-mail address to which any error reports will be e-mailed. If the WebserviceX.NET retrieval fails, an e-mail will be sent to this address. You may enter more than one e-mail address, separated by a comma.
- **Error Email Sender**: You can select the e-mail address from which the e-mail will be sent (these are set in the next panel, **Store Email Addresses**).
- **Error Email Template**: Choose the default template provided by Magento, or if you have created your own customized template (see `Chapter 8`, *Promotion and Communication*, regarding transactional e-mails), you may select that.

Store Email Addresses settings

Magento allows you to set up to five different e-mails for use throughout your store installation. You can set different e-mails at the Website and Store View levels as well.

For each e-mail, you have to set the following :

- **Sender Name**: The name that will appear in the **From** field of any e-mail sent by Magento
- **Sender Email**: The e-mail address used in the **From** field

Contacts settings

Magento has a built-in **Contact Us** form as part of its code. Use of this form is optional, as you may have another extension that provides more customization or functionality.

Contact Us

- **Enable Contact Us**: Set to **Yes** to enable the default Magento Contact Us form as shown in the preceding screenshot.

Email Options

- **Send Emails To**: Enter the e-mail address to which you would like the Contact Us form submissions e-mailed. You might choose to send them to a customer service rep in your organization or to an e-mail address that automatically ingests the inquiry into a **Customer Relationship management** (**CRM**) system, such as Salesforce Desk.
- **Email Sender**: Select your Store e-mail addresses that you wish as the sender of the e-mail.

 Unfortunately, you cannot set the Contact Us form submission to be sent from the submitter. Be aware of this, if you simply hit reply in your e-mail,the reply e-mail address will, by default, be the value of this field.

- **Email Template**: Choose the default **Contact Form** e-mail template, or a custom template you may have created (see Chapter 8, *Promotions and Communications*).

Reports settings

At present, there are only limited settings for affecting the overall reports in Magento, and these are only configurable at the global level.

Dashboard

- **Year-To-Date Starts**: Select the month and day you wish to use as the start of your "Year" for reporting purposes. You may choose to use a month and day that coincides with your fiscal year, not January 1.
- **Current Month Starts**: If you wish your reporting to start on a day other than the first of the month, you may select it here.

Content management settings

The static pages of your Magento store and the various content areas throughout the site are part of the **Content Management System** (**CMS**) of the platform. In Chapter 7, *Content and SEO*, we will go into more detail about how you can customize the content areas of your store.

WYSIWYG Options

WYSIWYG (pronounced "Wiz E Wig") stands for What You See Is What You Get, and refers to the idea that as you edit content on the site, you can use an editor that shows you what your content will look like as you write.

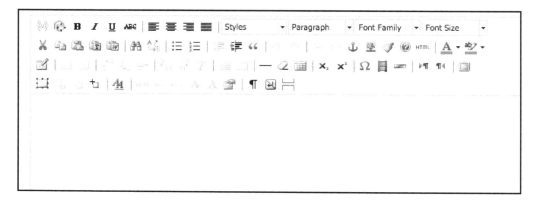

If you select text and click on the **B** (for bold) icon in the editor menu bar, your text will appear **bold**; if you click the **I**, you will see text in *italics*, and so forth.

- **Enable WYSIWYG Editor**: In some cases, you may not want to have the WYSIWYG editor used by default. If it is not engaged, the content field is simply a field that shows all text and HTML code. For those who prefer to input their own HTML code, disabling the WYSIWYG editor is preferred.
- **Use Static URLs for Media Content in WYSIWYG for Catalog**: In most cases, you'll want to leave this set to **No**. However, if you're inserting images into content fields for products and categories that require dedicated URLs which should not change if the Base URL changes, set this to **Yes**. An example would be when you're using another server to deliver the images, and you want to preserve that URL regardless of which Store View is being viewed on the frontend.

New Relic reporting

New Relic (http://newrelic.com/) is a popular, advanced server application monitoring system. Many developers and system administrators use New Relic to provide substantial information about the performance of server applications, including e-commerce systems.

Magento 2 includes an integration of New Relic for those who want this added level of performance monitoring. Check with your developer if you should use New Relic. Some hosting providers already perform 24/7 server monitoring, but few will provide the level of in-depth analysis that New Relic does.

Catalog panels

The settings in these panels affect the way your categories and products are displayed to consumers, the way you plan to manage inventory and availability, and how you push your product information to search engines and other parties.

Catalog settings

Product Fields Auto-Generation

Another new feature of Magento 2 is that you can now add placeholder fields and static copy to appear on product pages in the hidden **SEO meta tags**. We discuss SEO strategies and tools in Chapter 7, *Content and SEO*. These settings only apply to products that are **auto-generated**—that is, products that are not created individually, but are created by using variations from a single product (more on Products in Chapter 5, *Products*).

- **Mask for SKU**: Insert any placeholder code (such as {{name}} for Product Name) or characters you wish to use to auto-generate new SKUs (these can be changed after the product is created). If you want all the new SKUs to begin with NEW, you may enter NEW-{{name}}.
- **Mask for Meta Title**: Enter anything you wish to have auto-generated for the title meta field (this will appear as the page title in your browser).
- **Mask for Meta Keywords**: Enter whatever values you wish to use for auto-generated keywords.
- **Mask for Meta Description**: As will be discussed in Chapter 7, *Content and SEO*, the **Meta Description** field is an important field. By including the placeholders for product name and description, you should be creating unique Meta Descriptions for auto-generated products.

Product Reviews

When product reviews are active on your site (you can turn these off in the **Advanced Settings**, which we discuss later), you can choose whether to allow guests to write reviews or only allow logged-in users. In Chapter 4, *Preparing to Sell*, we discuss the difference between customer types.

Storefront

The settings here affect the way your products are shown in category listings or search results.

- **List Mode**: Products can be shown in a grid of rows and columns, or a list of products, one after the other. Choose the default view, and whether to allow users to switch between the views.
- **Products per Page on Grid Allowed Values**: On category pages, customers can choose the number of products to show in each view.

 So that the grid view doesn't end with a partial row of products, it's a good practice to choose multiples of how ever many products you are showing in a single row. For instance, if your products (according to your theme) are showing 4 in a row, you may want to use 8, 16, 24 as possible values (or 4, 8, 12, and so on). This would display 2, 4, and 6 rows, respectively.

- **Products per Page on Grid Default Value**: This is the default number of products to show in a Grid view. It does not have to be the lowest number used in the preceding field.
- **Products per Page on List Allowed Values**: Just as with the Grid View, you can choose the number of products customers may choose to view on each category page.
- **Products per Page on List Default Value**: The default number of products to display on a List View page.
- **Allow All Products Per Page**: Besides the allowed values noted before this, you can also allow customers to select to view "All" products. If your categories contain many products, you may not want to enable this, as it could make category page render times uncomfortably long.
- **Product Listing Sort by**: In each category, you can choose the position by which products will be shown (Position). Alternatively, you can set the default sort of products by **Name** or **Price**. Both will be in ascending order (A to Z, lowest to highest).

- **Use Flat Catalog Category/Use Flat Catalog Product**: One of the many ways Magento optimizes the installation for speed is to compile all the category and product information into two *flat* files for more rapid database lookups when rendering pages on your site. While you're setting up your new store, you may want to keep this set to **No** so that you won't have to re-index your site (see `Chapter 9`, *Security and Administration*, for more on indexing) while you're making lots of changes and updates to your content. When your store is live, you should set these to **Yes** to speed up your site.

- **Allow Dynamic Media URLs in Products and Categories**: As we addressed in the WYSIWYG Editor settings section earlier, you should allow Magento to create the full URL for media inserted into products and categories in order to keep from breaking image paths, especially if you're going to use multiple Store Views. While dynamic URLs can impact site performance, it's generally a better practice to have this turned on.
- **Swatches per Product**: Where you have product variations that include swatches—images of different colors, textures, and so on—you can limit the number of swatches that will appear on any product listing.

Product Alerts

You can allow customers to request e-mail alerts when a product price or availability changes. This can help you capture customers who are desperate for particular products, but willing to wait. Alert e-mails are generally sent out when Magento finds applicable changes (see the next panel for setting the frequency).

- **Allow Alert When Product Price Changes**: Enables the alert feature when a product price changes.
- **Price Alert Email Template**: Choose a default e-mail template or one you may have customized.
- **Allow Alert When Product Comes Back in Stock**: If a product shows "Out of Stock" on your store, a customer may request an e-mail alert when the product becomes available again.
- **Stock Alert Email Template**: Choose either the default or a customized e-mail template.
- **Alert Email Sender**: Choose your company e-mail contacts that the alert e-mail is to be sent from.

Product Alerts Run Settings

You have control over how often you want the alert e-mails to be sent.

 Periodic e-mails and other events in Magento are driven by a "cron" schedule—a server activity that occurs every so often (see the **Advanced Settings** for more on setting cron frequency). Despite the many cron-related settings in Magento, your developer needs to set your server to run the Magento cron functionality, ideally, every 5-10 minutes. If you set a cron-related activity, such as product alerts, and notice that it is not triggered properly, ask your developer to ensure that the Magento cron is running.

- **Frequency**: Set the alerts to be sent **Daily**, **Weekly**, or **Monthly**.
- **Start Time**: The time of day you wish the alerts to be sent. If you're using a **Daily** frequency, it should probably be set at a time after which any product updates have been made in Magento.
- **Error Email Recipient**: The address to which any error report is e-mailed if something doesn't go right with the product alerts function.
- **Error Email Sender**. The store contact from which the error e-mail is sent.
- **Error Email Template**: The default template or the one you have customized.

Product Image Placeholders

When you don't have images for a product, Magento can insert a placeholder image. By default, an image with the Magento logo will be used. Therefore, you should create "Coming Soon" placeholder images that complement your brand and design (and don't have the Magento logo).

The ideal size for each depends on your theme. Ask your developer to provide you with the ideal sizes if you wish to create your own placeholder images.

Recently Viewed/Compared Products

As customers click through your store, Magento remembers the products they are viewing and/or comparing.

- **Show for Current**: You can allow customers to see a list of their recent product views by **Website**, **Store**, or **Store View**, depending on how you have structured your multistore setup (this won't apply to Magento installations with only one Website/Store View).

- **Default Recently Viewed Products Count/Default Recently Compared Products Count**: Enter the number of products you wish to display in a list of recently viewed or compared items.

Product Video

With Magento 2, you can now add Vimeo or YouTube videos to your product listings (see `Chapter 5`, *Products*). In order to add YouTube videos, Google requires that you obtain a YouTube API key. For more information on the YouTube API, see `https://goo.gl/zaej4`.

Price

When you set a Base Currency (as described earlier in this chapter), you can decide if the Base Currency at the Global level will apply to all products, or if each website can apply a different Base Currency (the one associated with each website).

Layered Navigation

One of the most powerful features of Magento is that of "Layered Navigation"—the selectable filters that are usually seen along the left side of a category listing. They allow a customer to narrow the list of choices by selecting certain product attributes, such as color, model, and size.

Magento's layered navigation also shows, be default, a grouping of price ranges, such as $0-100, $100-500, and so on.

- **Display Product Count**: Enabling this feature will add the number of products that match a particular price range or attribute.
- **Price Navigation Step Calculation**: Magento 2 gives you three ways of calculating the price ranges displayed in the layered navigation: **Automatic (equalize price ranges)** will create price ranges by taking the least amount and the highest amount among the products shown, and creating equal groupings according to a set algorithm. **Automatic (equalize product counts)** uses the same method, but groups prices by creating equal numbers of products. When selecting this option, you will be allowed to choose whether each price interval will be shown as one price or a range, and the minimum number of products that will make up a single price interval. Finally, **Manual** gives you control over the dollar amount of each price step and the number of price intervals.

Catalog Search

Searching for products and categories within your store will be a common activity of customers. Understanding how search works can be complex though, unless you're familiar with how databases work. Consult with your developer on how to best help your customers search your site.

Besides the native search within the **MySQL** database that powers Magento, there are other search engines that can be employed as well as third-party solutions that can give your users better, faster results.

Search Engine Optimization

In `Chapter 7`, *Content and SEO*, we discuss the strategies for managing the SEO features of Magento. We will revisit this panel then, but for now, let's briefly describe each of the fields.

In Magento, the URL Key is that portion of the URL that designates the product, category, or page.
In `http://www.yourstore.com/motor-boats`, "motor-boats" is the URL Key for the Motor Boats category. Likewise,
for `http://www.yourstore.com/iphone-5-case`, "iphone-5-case" is the URL Key for that product. If the URL ends in `.html`, the `.html` is not considered part of the URL Key.

- **Popular Search Terms**: As customers visit your store, Magento can record any of their searches. If enabled, you can view the top searches each day in the Dashboard of your backend. Customers can also go to a *Search Terms* page, and see what are the most popular search terms.
- **Product URL Suffix/Category URL Suffix**: You can enter whatever you wish to appear after a product URL. Usually, you would use **html** (a dot before suffix is added automatically), or leave it blank.
- **Using Categories Path for Product URLs**: You can choose to include or not include the name of the category in the product URL: `http://www.yourstore.com/kids-shoes/running/great-shoe.html` versus `http://www.yourstore.com/great-shoe.html`.
- **Create Permanent Redirect for URLs if URL Key Changed**: When you change the URL Key for a category or product, the old key no longer points to the new page. If the old category or product key is listed in search engines or links to your site from other websites, visitors clicking those links would see a "404 – File Not Found" error. If you want old keys to "re-point" to the new key, enable this feature.

- **Page Title Separator**: If you have entered title suffixes or prefixes under **General | Design** earlier, you can specify a separator that you may want to appear between the actual page title and the suffix or prefix. "-" or "|" are common separators.
- **Use Canonical Link Meta Tag for Categories/Products**: A canonical link tells the actual primary URL of a page to Google and other search engines. For instance, if you assign a chair to the "furniture" and "seating" categories in your site, it might be possible for customers to access the chair at `http://www.yourdomain.com/chair.html`, `http://www.yourdomain.com/furniture/chair.html`, or `http://www.yourdomain.com/seating/chair.html`. If a search engine indexed all these URLs, you would be penalized for having duplicate content. Yet, if the canonical link for each one were `http://www.yourdomain.com/chair.html`, the search engine would consider all three pages to actually be the same page and not duplicates of each other.

Category Top Navigation

The main navigation menu on your site will, depending on your design, show categories in a hierarchical fashion. That is, there will be a top level of categories with sub-menus showing lower sub-categories. You can control the maximum number of levels that will be shown. Setting this value to means the menu will show all levels possible.

Downloadable Product Options

Many online stores today sell digital products such as music, books, and software. Magento gives you great flexibility in selling these intangibles, as we'll discuss later in `Chapter 5`, *Products*.

- **Order Item Status to Enable Downloads**: Depending on your order workflow, you may want to allow customers to receive links for their downloads as soon as they place their order. Otherwise, they will be e-mailed links (and have them show up in their own Dashboard) once the payment is processed and the order is invoiced (more on orders workflow in `Chapter 4`, *Preparing to Sell*).
- **Default Maximum Number of Downloads**: You can restrict the number of times a customer may download a digital product. Setting this to gives them unlimited downloads.
- **Shareable**: Can users share their download link with others? If not, set this to **No**.

- **Default Sample Title**: Magento lets you include samples for downloading on a product detail page. This can be useful if you want to give a customer one chapter of a book or a snippet of an audio file. This field value will be the name you give to these sample links.
- **Default Link Title**: Likewise, you can set the title used for download links.
- **Open Links in New Window**: For download links displayed in a customer's Dashboard, you may want clicking the link to open a new window rather than refreshing the user's screen. This behavior largely depends on the browser used.
- **Use Content-Disposition**: Your selection here determines whether clicking on a link will open the file in the browser (**inline**), or force the browser to save the file to the user's computer (**attachment**).
- **Disable Guest Checkout if Cart Contains Downloadable Items**: If you allow a customer to check out as a Guest, they will not be creating a Customer Account in Magento, and therefore, will not be able to log in to retrieve their downloads. Guests will only be able to download from the e-mails they receive.

To give your customers maximum flexibility—and to better control access to downloadable items—you should disable Guest Checkout.

Date & Time Custom Options.

You can set certain parameters when date selections are shown to customers.

- **Use JavaScript Calendar**: For date entry fields, using a JavaScript calendar will display a clickable calendar rather than only allowing a text entry.

To help customers enter dates more accurately, a JavaScript pop-up calendar can be a tremendous aid.

- **Date Fields Order**: Like so many things in life, people in different regions of the world read dates in different orders. In the US, the "normal" order is Month-Day-Year. In many other countries, the order is Day-Month-Year. Some may even prefer Year-Month-Day.
- **Time Format:** You can choose to display time in a 12-hour or 24-hour format.
- **Year Range**: Set the minimum and maximum year you want any entered dates to fall between. You may, for instance, not want entered dates prior to the current year.

Inventory settings

If you sell tangible products, you want your customers to purchase items knowing whether that product is in stock or not. Furthermore, your accounting depends on maintaining accurate inventory counts, as much of your capital may be tied up in stock.

 If you dropship your orders-that is, you send your orders to a distributor who maintains inventory and ships directly to your consumers-it may be difficult, even impossible, to maintain accurate inventory levels. Distributors have to ship for many retailers, and without real-time integrations, you won't be able to accurately display stock levels to your customers.

We'll cover inventory management and the process of accounting for orders in Chapter 5, *Products*. Many of the settings in this panel can be overridden at the product level: consider these more as default settings.

Stock Options

- **Set Items' Status to be In Stock When Order is Cancelled**: When an order is cancelled, Magento "releases" the items in the order. If you want those items to increase inventory counts, any product which went "Out of Stock" as a result of that order can be changed back to "In Stock" as a status.
- **Decrease Stock When Order is Placed**: Related, do you want an order that is not yet fulfilled to reduce the available inventory stock?
- **Display Out of Stock Products**: If you have products that go out of stock, but return to In Stock quickly, you may want to leave them visible to consumers. This gives interested buyers the opportunity-if enabled, as discussed earlier-to sign up for a product availability alert. This can help gauge interest for replenishment.

 Setting **Display Out of Stock** to **No** will not completely hide the product. Unless you set the product's visibility to hidden or disable the product, it can still be directly accessed by it's URL. Setting this field to **No** will remove it from listing in categories.

- **Only X left Threshold**: If you set this number to greater than 0, a message will appear to customers when the stock level of a product reaches that number or less. For example, if you enter **10**, when the product inventory count declines to 10 or below, the customer will see "Only 10 left." This could be a good incentive to buyers who might consider this message to denote high demand for an item.
- **Display products availability in stock in the frontend**: Enabling this feature will display whether products are In Stock or Out of Stock, whichever the case may be, on the product detail screen.

Product Stock Options

- **Manage Stock**: Do you want to manage your inventory counts in Magento? If so, choose **Yes**.

- **Backorders**: This Global setting affects how you allow customers to place orders for products that are out of stock. If you want to allow backorders, you can simply take the order or select to take the order, *and* let the customer know by a message on the Shopping Cart that the item is backordered.

- **Maximum Qty Allowed in Shopping Cart**: We've never had a client choose any lesser value than the default of 10,000 items. However, we can certainly see where it might be prudent to limit the number of items of any one product that can be purchased. Particularly if you want to restrict purchases by resellers.

- **Out-of-Stock Threshold**: While it's understandable that if a product's inventory count goes to 0, it would be out of stock, you might want to keep a minimum amount in stock as a cushion.

- **Minimum Qty Allowed in Shopping Cart**: This sub-panel allows you to create minimum purchase quantities based on Customer Group (see `Chapter 4`, *Preparing to Sell*, for more on Customer Groups). For example, you might want to require that wholesalers purchase a minimum of 12 of any item.

- **Notify for Quantity Below**: During Magento's cron operation, it can send an e-mail notifying of any products whose inventory count falls below the entered amount.

- **Enable Qty Increments**: If you set this to **Yes**, you can set the default increments at which products will be sold. If you want to sell your products in groups of 3, then customers would be limited to buying 3, 6, 9, and so on of a product.

- **Automatically Return Credit Memo Item to Stock**: When you refund a customer for a returned item, Magento can automatically return the item to the inventory count.

 Usually, Credit Memos-or refunds-are made when an item is returned, damaged, or lost in transit. In any of these cases, you will most likely need to manually adjust inventory accordingly. Setting this field to **No** is the most common choice.

XML Sitemap settings

The sitemap is an XML file that is accessible to search engines to help them index the contents of your site. Rather than forcing Google, for instance, to learn all about your site by following all the links in your site, a well-formed sitemap can provide Google with links to *all* the content in your site within one file.

We will discuss the relevancy of this panel and its settings in Chapter 7, *Content and SEO*, when we cover SEO optimization.

RSS Feeds settings

Rich Site Summary (**RSS**) feeds are as widely used today as they were earlier. News readers were very common in the early years of the Web to retrieve and display timely information from websites.

That said, making your website information available via RSS feeds may help publicize what you have to offer should any services subscribe. Additionally, RSS feeds can be used by your resellers, for instance, to keep them alerted to new wholesale products you're offering.

Email to a Friend settings

Another neat marketing feature of Magento is the ability for your customers to easily e-mail links of products to their friends. This can help expose your products to a wider audience of referred consumers: a virtual "word-of-mouth" market.

The settings in this panel are designed to help you control the frequency of these e-mails, as it could be easy for someone to overuse this to spam their friends or others, thereby damaging your store's reputation.

Customers panels

Of course, you don't succeed unless you have customers. They're the buyers that make e-commerce fruitful. We'll discuss more about customers in Chapter 4, *Preparing to Sell*, but for now, let's quickly touch on the various settings that aid your interaction with your buyers.

Newsletter settings

Subscription Options

Once you have a buyer, you should work to keep them interested in your store, as it's less expensive to resell to current customers than to find and attract new ones. Magento helps by providing an e-mail newsletter functionality where you can compose and e-mail promotional messages to customers who give you permission to do so.

There are many reasons you should investigate alternatives to Magento for sending out newsletters. It's not that Magento's newsletter functionality is bad—it's just not as good as many affordable third-party services. Plus, you don't run the risk of overwhelming your server's mail sender or having your site *blacklisted* by providers who might consider your e-mails as spam. Our favorite one, which integrates very well with Magento, is MailChimp. In addition, MailChimp's Magento extension (`htt p://store.ebizmarts.com/magemonkey-magento2.html`) can add a mailing service called Mandrill to your store that adds abandoned cart e-mails and other low-cost features for increasing communication with your customers.

The options in this panel give you control over the e-mail templates used for confirming subscriptions and unsubscribes. Additionally, you can set whether you want subscribers to confirm their actions, which can help reduce rejections as spam.

Customer Configuration settings

Online Customers Options

Under the **Customers** menu in the main navigation menu on the left, you can go to **Now Online** to see all the customers currently on your site. Visitors will pause as they go through your site to read product information, look at category listings, and so on. Whether they're considered "online" is determined by the amount of time between clicks or actions. By default, if a customer doesn't perform an action on your site for 15 minutes or more, they are no longer considered to be online. You can increase or decrease this time interval according to your preference.

This interval is not the same as the User Sessions counted by Google Analytics, as that is determined by settings in Google, and is affected by the user's IP address, Google login, and many other factors. This is just for your real-time view as to who is on your site at any given moment.

Account Sharing Options

You can choose whether your registered customers will automatically be assigned to all websites in your Magento installation or only to the websites to which they register. If your websites are quite different in scope, or if they cater to different types of consumers, you may want to restrict customer accounts to each website.

As we will cover more thoroughly in Chapter 4, *Preparing to Sell*, customers in Magento are those who register either by creating a customer account or by registering during checkout. Guest customers are not listed in the Customers section of your site, as they are not considered customers in Magento. In other words, customers are those who are registered and can log into your site.

Create New Account Options

As customers register with your site, you can choose to automatically assign them to a customer group based on a customer VAT tax qualification. In the US, VAT taxes are not relevant. We will cover the creation of VAT tax rules in Chapter 4, *Preparing to Sell*.

- **Enable Automatic Assignment to Customer Group**: By selecting **Yes**, you will be given the opportunity to assign customers to various groups based on their VAT tax entry.
- **Default Group**: New customer registrations that are not addressed by VAT tax considerations will be automatically assigned to the group selected.
- **Default Value for Disable Automatic Group Changes Based on VAT ID**: If this is enabled, the customer group changes automatically for customers who enter a VAT ID. If disabled, customers are assigned to the Default Group and can later be reassigned by an administrator.
- **Show VAT Number on Frontend**: Setting this to **Yes** will show the VAT ID number to customers on your website.
- **Default Email Domain**: This is one of the more unusual fields in Magento, as it has never had any effect on how we have operated Magento stores in the past. What it appears to do, however, is to create a temporary e-mail address for orders until the customer completes the checkout process. This is one setting you can most likely ignore.
- **Default Welcome Email**: Choose the e-mail template or customized e-mail that you wish to send to new registered customers.
- **Default Welcome Email Without Password**: You can choose an alternative e-mail template for accounts that are created without a password.
- **Email Sender**: To set the address from which you wish the welcome e-mail to be sent.
- **Require Emails Confirmation**: If you want to validate your customer's e-mail address, Magento can send an e-mail asking them to click on a link to validate their e-mail. Doing so can help to reduce communication errors due to mistyped e-mail addresses.

As with e-mail newsletter subscriptions, some may think that sending confirmation e-mails are a bit much; that customers will be turned off by receiving additional e-mails. We feel just the opposite: confirmation e-mails not only demonstrate to your customers that you want to confirm their decision, it allows you an additional way to send a marketing message to your customers. Why not include a coupon opportunity or new product announcement in your confirmation e-mails? There's nothing that says you can't use these as upsell opportunities.

- **Confirmation Link Email**: A standard or custom e-mail template for the e-mail confirmation message.
- **Welcome Email**: If you do require a confirming e-mail, the template you choose here will be sent to customers after they have confirmed their e-mail address.
- **Generate Human-Friendly Customer ID**: By default, Magento creates a random, complex ID for customer records. You can have Magento create IDs that are less "geeky", especially if you want your customers to use their ID for communicating with you.

Password Options

To provide better service to your registered customers, Magento provides a solid means of allowing customers to reset their passwords if they forget it. This can often happen if a customer revisits your site after some time. Rather than subject your valued customers to a litany of silly questions (for example, "Who was your first grade teacher?"), Magento simply e-mails them a link to reset their password.

To retrieve their password, they will have to use the e-mail address with which they registered. Another good reason to enable e-mail confirmations.

- **Forgot Email Template**: Choose the default or custom template that you wish to send to users who have forgotten their password.
- **Remind Email Template**: The chosen template here sends the password to the customer; generally, once they register an account.
- **Reset Password Template**: This e-mail tells the customer that their password has been reset.
- **Password Template Email Sender**: Select the store contact from whom password-related e-mails will be sent.
- **Recovery Link Expiration Period (days)**: You should limit the "life" of a password reset link for security purposes.

Name and Address Options

Magento gives you flexibility in how you wish to obtain the name and address information from your customers when they register or purchase on your site.

- **Number of Lines in a Street Address**: The default number of address fields is two, but you may choose to show one to four lines if you like.
- **Show Prefix**: This refers to name prefixes, such as Dr., Mr., or Ms.
- **Prefix Dropdown Options**: If you enable prefixes, you can enter the ones you wish to provide to customers in a dropdown by listing them, separated by a semicolon (;). For example, you could enter `Mr.;, Ms.;, Dr.; Hon.;, Rev.`". If you leave this blank, the prefix field will be a simple text entry field where the customer can enter whatever they like.
- **Show Middle Name (initial)**: Choose **Yes** if you wish to provide a middle initial field.
- **Show Suffix**: Like the prefix, you can allow the use of name suffixes, such as "Jr.", "II", or "Esq."
- **Suffix Dropdown Options**: Using a semicolon as a separator, enter whatever suffixes you wish to appear in a drop-down menu. Whenever we have enabled suffixes in the past, we've simply left this blank to allow customers to enter anything they wish, as there are so many available choices.
- **Show Date of Birth**: This is a field that can sometimes be a bit intrusive (much like Gender, as discussed further in this section). If you do want to obtain customer birth dates for the purpose of marketing or validating adult status, enable this field.
- **Show Tax/VAT Number**: Enable this field if you need to ask customers to enter their VAT ID. If you're creating group rules based on VAT, as described earlier, then you would most likely enable this field.
- **Show Gender**: As with the birth date, it's best to have a legitimate reason to ask this, as some customers may feel this is a bit overreaching.

Login Options

This section has one simple choice: to direct registered customers to their account dashboard after they log in, or return them to the page from which they came when first accessing their account.

Address Templates

The template code shown here dictates how addresses will be displayed to your customers on the site or text-only e-mail (**Text** and **Text One Line**), in an HTML email (HTML) or on a PDF, such as a printed invoice.

The code uses substitution tags to render the information. Adding a `return` after the line of code will insert a line break in the final display.

It's easy to break your layouts if you don't know what you're doing. Given that this involves knowledge of Magento programming variables, you may be better-off consulting with your Magento developer should you need to modify your address layouts.

CAPTCHA

A CAPTCHA is an image that appears at the bottom of a form, where the user is asked to type the characters shown in order to proceed.

CAPTCHAs are designed to thwart scripts that rapidly try combinations of names and passwords to crack into a website. It can also hinder hackers who try to set up user accounts automatically. Although they're not entirely foolproof (there are some services that use humans to assist ne'er-do-wells when encountering CAPTCHAs), you do want to protect your customers as much as possible.

If you enable CAPTCHAs, you will be given several choices for configuring how they will work on your site.

- **Font**: If more than one font is shown in the dropdown (early versions of Magento 2 only included *LinLibertine*), you can select different fonts to text for readability.
- **Forms**: Select the forms on which you wish to include a CAPTCHA. We usually enable CAPTCHAs on the Create User, Login, Forgot Password, and Contact Us forms. Customers who are checking out are not hackers, as these criminals wouldn't bother buying something just to create multiple accounts.

- **Displaying Mode**: For the Login form, you can choose to show the CAPTCHA always or whenever someone fails to enter the correct username and password after a number of attempts.
- **Number of Unsuccessful Attempts to Login**: Enter the number of failed login attempts that will trigger the use of a CAPTCHA.
- **CAPTCHA Timeout (minutes)**: As an additional measure of security, you can limit the amount of time for which a CAPTCHA is valid.
- **Number of Symbols**: You can enter any value from 1 to 8, as well as a range (for example, 2-4). A range will randomly choose the number of characters shown within the range you designate.
- **Symbols Use in CAPTCHA**: The default selection provided by Magento is a solid choice, as it removes those characters that are hard to distinguish from one another, such as "I", "l", and "1".
- **Case Sensitive**: If you want users to enter letter characters using the same case (upper or lower) as shown, you can enable this feature. We usually allow either case, as long as the customer enters the correct letter.

Wish List settings

Many retailers like to provide a *wish list* to customers, as it helps them build a selection of products they want to buy at some time in the future. Customer wish lists can also be accessed by you should the customer call to place their order, thus saving time and showing the customer that you're on top of things.

You should be aware that to create a wish list, a customer must create a registered customer account, and be logged in. This is the only way a wish list can be saved and attributed to a customer for later retrieval.

 Wish List functionality in Magento has previously been limited to the Enterprise edition. As of this writing, it is appearing in the Magento 2 Community Edition. If you don't see this section in your backend, it may have been moved to the Enterprise edition, or you might have this module turned off in the **Advanced** section.

General Options

In this panel, you can enable or disable the wish list functionality on your store or stores.

Share Options

These settings affect the way wish lists are shared by customers with others. Customers can choose to have their wish list e-mailed to multiple recipients.

- **Email Sender**: Select the store contact from whom the shared wish list will be sent.
- **Email Template**: Choose the default or customized e-mail template for the outgoing e-mail.
- **Max Emails Allowed to be Sent**: Enter the maximum number of recipients you will allow for the e-mails. You may not want to allow a huge number, as it could be considered spamming.
- **Email Text Length Limit**. With each list, the customer can enter a message to include for their recipients. This number is the maximum number of characters (not words) you allow.

My Wish List Link

A wish list is much like a shopping cart, except that it isn't used for checking out. Like a shopping cart display (see **My Cart Link** under **Sales | Checkout** later in this chapter), you can choose to display the number of different items in the wish list or the total quantity of products.

For example, if the list has one cap and two of the same shirt, you could choose to show 2 (**Display number of items in wish list**) or 3 (**Display item quantities**).

Promotions settings

In Chapter 7, *Content and SEO*, we'll learn how to create promotional discounts. This section allows you to set the default parameters for creating coupon codes.

Auto Generated Specific Coupon Codes

- **Code Length**: The number of characters you should have in a coupon code.

 It's not necessary to have long coupon codes in order to create large numbers of random coupon codes. For example, if you choose the **Alphanumeric** code format (discussed further in this section) and a length of six characters, you could create as many as 2,176,783,336 possible combinations (36^6: A-Z, plus 0-9 for 6 places). That would provide a unique coupon code to about one-third of all the people on Earth! Shorter codes are easier for your customers to type without making mistakes.

- **Code Format**: Choose between alphanumeric (A-Z, 0-9), alphabetical (A-Z), or numeric (0-9) as the characters to use when generating random codes.
- **Code Prefix**: Enter any value you wish to have at the beginning of a coupon code. Avoid spaces.
- **Code Suffix**: As with the prefix, enter the value you want at the end of a coupon code. You might use either of these to denote codes that belong to a particular store or campaign.
- **Dash Every X Characters**: Magento can insert a dash every X number of characters. For instance, if you set this at 3 and have a code length of 9, a code might look like DJI-9EF-PL7.

Persistent Shopping Cart settings

When people visit your website, Magento creates a number of cookies in their browser to help keep track of the customers' use of your store. You can enable *persistence* to allow Magento to remember a customer's shopping cart contents well beyond their initial visit to your site. Magento does this by creating a record in its database of the cart contents so that if the user revisits your site using the same browser (like Chrome, Safari, Firefox, and IE), they will find that the shopping cart has retained their chosen items.

Persistence also pertains to maintaining a customer's **login state**, or whether or not they have logged into your site as a registered customer.

- **Enable Persistence**: **Yes** to enable; **No** to disable.
- **Persistence Lifetime (seconds)**: Enter the length of time you wish to retain a customer's cart contents or their login state. The default of **31536000** is 60 years, which is probably more than you need.
- **Enable "Remember Me"**: When a customer logs into your site, they can check a Remember Me box so that they will not have to log in again as long as they revisit your site with the persistence lifetime.

> If you feel that your customer's information is sensitive-or perceived to be sensitive-you may want to enter a low persistence lifetime period and/or disable the Remember Me functionality.

- **"Remember Me" Default Value**: If you have enabled the "Remember Me" feature, you can choose if you want it checked (**Yes**) or unchecked (**No**), by default. We recommend you leave it unchecked for security purposes, as it then forces the customer to determine as to whether to make their login status available on their computer.

- **Clear Persistence on Log Out**: If enabled, when a logged-in customer purposely logs out of your website, their shopping cart and state will be erased.
- **Persist Shopping Cart**: If you wish to have Magento remember customers' shopping cart contents, enable this setting.

Sales panels

The Sales panelsaddress the configurations related to the checkout process, and the way orders are managed in your system. These are important and critical settings, as they can greatly determine how your customers are actually able to purchase what you're selling.

Sales settings

General

The onlychoice on this panel is whether or not to show a customer's **IP number** when you view their orders, invoices, shipment, and the like. An IP number is the numerical ID assigned to all computers and devices on the Internet. Your computer has an IP number, although to the world, your IP number may be that of your router or gateway. An IP number, such as 66.211.190.110, is unique to each connected device.

Why would an IP be important to know? In most cases, it isn't. However, it can help you analyze the *legitimacy* of an order. For instance, if you suspect that an order is not "honest," you can do a *lookup* of the IP number for clues about the buyer (try http://ip-lookup.net/). For example, if the buyer's address is in the US, but their IP number shows a location in Nigeria, the order might have been created using a stolen credit card. Not that Nigerians are thieves, but when a customer is not accessing your store from the same side of the globe as their billing address, it might be suspect.

There are a number of services that provide a form of insurance for your orders by comparing the order parameters against a variety of factors such as IP location. Signify'd (https://www.signifyd.com) is one that we've used with great success. Signify'd analyzes each order, and if it is approved it, the order is validated and the payment method charged. If not, Signify'd can optionally cancel the order automatically. Once it approves an order, and if the order later turns out to be purchased using a stolen card, or if the buyer disputes the charges, Signify'd reimburses you for any loss and charges.

Checkout Totals Sort Order

You can manage the order in which the various totals and amounts are listed on the checkout screen. Enter any numbers in these fields. The sort order is based on the item with the lowest number, working up.

Reorder

For many retailers, customers often order the same thing over and over again. If you turn on **Reorder**, you will allow registered customers to use any past order as a new order.

Invoice and Packing Slip Design

In your Magento backend, you can choose to download a PDF of an invoice or packing slip, or view these in a new browser window (and later print it). By default, Magento will use the logo image you uploaded in the **General | Design** panel. In this panel, you can upload logo files that are of higher resolution or a more compatible height-to-width ratio. You'll have to experiment to find the ideal logo size and quality, but if you're going to e-mail PDF invoices or print packing slips for your packages, it's worth the effort.

You can also enter the address (or other information) you wish to appear at the top underneath your logo.

Minimum Order Amount

You may have the need to require a minimum order amount per order. Sometimes wholesalers require minimum order amounts. In other cases, we've had clients who have minimum requirements, because they offered some low-cost parts or small items: if a customer orders one small $2 part, the client would lose money processing the order. A minimum order amount can be set to make sure the smallest orders meet your baseline costs.

- **Enable**: Choose to enforce a minimum order level.
- **Minimum Amount**: Enter the minimum order total allowed after any discount has been applied, but before shipping and taxes.
- **Include Tax to Amount**: You can choose to include taxes in the minimum amount calculation.
- **Description Message**: Enter what you wish to communicate to your customers in cases where their shopping cart total does not meet the minimum order level.
- **Error to Show in Shopping Cart**: If a customer clicks on the "Proceed to Checkout" button, but has a cart total less than your minimum order amount, the text of this field will be displayed as an error message.

- **Validate Each Address Separately in Multi-address Checkout**: In `Chapter 4`, *Preparing to Sell*, we will describe how multi-address checkouts work. By enabling this setting, you can choose to apply the minimum order amount against each delivery address. If disabled, your minimum total level will be measured only against the entire order, regardless of which items are shipped to various addresses.
- **Multi-address Description Message**: For multiple address shipments, enter what you wish to explain to customers about your minimum order policy.
- **Multi-address Error to Show in Shopping Cart**: As described previously, you can enter the error message you wish to display when a shopper attempts to checkout with multiple destinations, and their order fails to meet your minimum order specifications.

Dashboard

The single configuration in this panel allows you to set whether or not to use real-time calculated data on your backend dashboard. If enabled, Magento will keep running totals on your store activity that are periodically updated, but not in real-time.

When you're starting out, you can probably use real-time data. However, if you have a busy store-and depending on your server configuration-you may find it less taxing on your Magento system to use *aggregated data*.

Orders Cron Settings

In previous versions of Magento, orders where payment was being processed could be stuck in the "processing" status for a very long time. By setting a limit here, orders that are pending payment can expire after a period of time.

 If you're using checks or money orders for payment methods, you may want to set this to a sufficient time to allow for receipt of these payments.

Gift Options

It's not uncommon for many retailers-especially those selling gifts, flowers, jewelry, and so on-to allow customers to include a *gift message* with their order. Gift messages, if allowed, can be offered to customers at either or both of two levels: order and item. An **order level gift message** is one that is applied to the entire order, and will appear on the packing slip as a single comment. **Order item level gift messages** can be added for each item in the shopping cart, and will appear next to the item description on the packing slip.

The native gift message functionality will not print on gift cards without customization of your Magento code. By default, gift messages appear on the packing slip.

Minimum Advertised Price

If you sell name-brand products, you will no doubt encounter the concept of MAP (Minimum Advertised Price). Generally, manufacturers or distributors may require you to only show MAP prices to consumers who visit your store. Many will allow you to sell at a lower price, but only if you hide the actual price; they may also require that the customer performs some action in order to have the true price revealed. Some manufacturers will never allow the display of a lower price, in which case, you should *not* enable the functionality of this feature. Simply use the MAP price as the MSRP price for a product.

- **Enable MAP**: You can globally enable the MAP functionality. Once enabled, MAP rules can be set or overridden at the product detail level. Therefore, even if you only need the MAP functionality for a single product, you have to first enable it here.
- **Display Actual Price**: You can choose how you reveal the actual price to your consumers. **On Gesture** will add a "Click for Price" link with a popup showing the discounted price as well as an explanation as to why you cannot show the actual price on the category listing. **In Cart** will display the actual price in the customer's shopping cart, and **Before Order Confirmation** means that the real price will only be displayed at the end of the checkout process, but before the customer completes their purchase.
- **Default Popup Text Message**: When you have MAP enabled, a "Click for price" link will appear if you have chosen **On Gesture** in the preceding field. The message you wish to show in this popup box can be entered here. You can use basic HTML tags, such as `<br />`, for a line break.
- **Default "What's This" Text Message**: Where you are not revealing the price until the Cart or Order Confirmation stages, a "What's this?" link will appear, and will display the text in this field.

Sales Emails settings

As you process orders, your customers may expect e-mails to confirm their order, be notified about updates, and receive shipment notifications. This panel helps you configure these e-mails.

General Settings

In Magento 1.x, any action you took to send an e-mail to a customer would have to wait until the e-mail was processed and sent. While this might take nothing but seconds, Magento 2 allows you to set sending actions asynchronously, meaning that the sending function would happen by itself without causing you to wait before having your screen update.

For the remaining e-mails, the following settings are the same:

- **Enabled**: You don't have to send each e-mail. Only enable the ones you wish to have sent to your customers.
- **Email Sender**: Select the store contact you wish to have as the sending e-mail name and address.
- **Template**: Choose the default or customized template that will be used for the relevant e-mail message.
- **Template for Guest**: If a customer checks out as a "Guest," the chosen template will be used.
- **Send Email Copy To**: You can include a list of additional e-mail recipients, each separated by a comma. If you want to get a copy of what your customers see, enter your own personal e-mail address.
- **Send Email Copy Method**: You can choose to have the additional copies sent as **Blind Carbon Copies** (**BCC**) or as separate e-mails, each addressed to the recipients listed in the preceding field.

PDF Print-outs settings

In your Magento backend, you can download invoices, shipments, and credit memos as PDFs. If you want the order ID or number shown in the head of each, you can enable it here.

Tax settings

The rules and conditions for applying tax rates will be explained in Chapter 4, *Preparing to Sell*. Here we want to address the default tax classes for your store(s), and how taxes will be applied and displayed to your customers.

Tax Classes

Here you can select any listed tax class that you wish to assign as the default for shipping, products, and customers.

Calculation Settings

Each jurisdiction has rules for how taxes are to be calculated on orders. Some require calculation on the order total or on each individual item; others may want prices displayed to include applicable taxes; and you may be required to apply taxes on pre-discounted prices.

You should consult with your tax advisor for rules relating to your own taxing jurisdiction(s).

Default Tax Destination Calculation

While actual taxes are managed by the tax rules you enter elsewhere (see `Chapter 4`, *Preparing to Sell*), you can set a default taxing jurisdiction, including state and postal code.

Price Display Settings

In the US, it is a common practice to display prices and shipping *without* including taxes. In some countries, it is more common to display prices including taxes. You can specify your preference here.

Shopping Cart Display Settings/Orders, Invoices, Credit Memo Display Settings

As with product prices, you can specify how you wish to display taxes in a customer's shopping cart, orders, invoices, and credit memos. The default settings are common for US-based retailers.

Fixed Product Taxes

In some parts of the world, products are sold with fixed taxes. If that applies to your business, you can enable **Fixed Product Taxes** (**FPT**), and specify how you wish to have them displayed.

Checkout settings

When a customer is ready to buy, you have to provide the processes and features that will help them complete their purchase.

Checkout Options

- **Enable One page Checkout**: When enabled (default setting), your customers will see a **Proceed to Checkout** button on their shopping cart. If disabled, they will only have the ability to use the multi-step, multi-address checkout method.

- **Allow Guest Checkout**: You may allow customers to checkout without creating a customer account.

  It's very common for retailers to assume that a Guest Checkout is less intimidating to customers, and therefore, less likely to turn away customers. However, without registering, customers cannot look up previous orders or utilize previous billing and shipping addresses. The only difference between guest checkout and registered customers' checkout is one additional field: password. We've never seen this one field keep customers from checking out. The key, we have found, is to edit the headings on the first checkout page panel to read "New Customer?" and "Existing Customer?" instead of "Register to Create an Account" and "Returning Customers?" This change sounds much friendlier and requires much less consideration by your shoppers.

- **Require Customer To Be Logged In To Checkout**: If you disable Guest Checkout, you can choose whether to require customers to be logged-in before purchasing. If a new customer registers-and this setting is enabled-they will need to confirm their account, and then log in to continue the checkout process. This can be important if you are offering discounts or special pricing to your registered customers.
- **Enable Terms and Conditions**: As an added measure of security and sound practice, you can display checkout terms and conditions during the checkout process, even requiring customers to affirm their acceptance (see Chapter 4, *Preparing to Sell*, for more on setting up Terms and Conditions).

Shopping Cart

- **Quote Lifetime (days)**: When an order for which payment has not yet been obtained is created in Magento, such as in the case of a Purchase Order or Check/Money Order, the prices included in the order will be saved for the length of time entered here.
- **After Adding a Product Redirect to Shopping Cart**: As customers click the **Add to Cart** button on a page, they can either remain on the same page, or be automatically taken to the Shopping Cart page.

We will go into great detail about product types in Chapter 5, *Products*, and then the image choices for Grouped and Configurable products may make more sense. In short, however, you are choosing whether to show the main image for a group or configurable product, or the image of the *child product* actually selected.

My Cart Link

Choose if you would rather show the number of different products in a shopper's cart or the total number of individual quantities selected. **Display number of items in cart** will count the number of different items or SKUs in the cart (for example, 1 cap and 2 baseballs would show "2" as the number of items), whereas **Display item quantities** will add up all item quantities (for example, 1 cap and 2 baseballs would total 3 items).

Shopping Cart Sidebar

If your design theme allows, you can elect to show in the page sidebar a "mini-cart" of items in the shopper's cart. You can also limit the number of items shown to a number of the most recent additions.

Payment Failed Emails

If a customer checks out with a payment method that fails, you can have a notice sent to someone in your company. You can use this information, if you choose, to contact the purchaser, and help them complete the sale. Sometimes, a customer may not enter information correctly, and therefore, fail to use a valid payment method. Your intervention may help to complete a purchase. On the other hand, multiple failures may indicate that someone is trying multiple credit cards that were stolen in the hope that one will work.

Shipping settings

Unless you're selling digital products or services, you will have products to ship to your customers. This simple panel provides fields for indicating the origin address of your shipments, which will be used to calculate shipping rates.

If you're shipping from multiple locations-such as multiple warehouses or distributors-you will need to investigate additional solutions to provide multiple origin addresses if you plan on using real-time shipping rates for your customers. If you use fixed shipping rates, multiple origin addresses are not necessary.

You can also specify a text message about your shipping policy that will be displayed to your customers. For example, you might want to let your customer know that "orders will ship within 3-5 business days, then delivered by the method selected during checkout".

Multi-shipping settings

One of Magento's best-kept secrets is its ability to allow a customer to take a single shopping cart, and ship portions of the order to multiple addresses.

 When a customer chooses to ship to multiple addresses, they cannot check out as a Guest. Customer registration is required in order to record and manage multiple shipping destinations.

On this panel, you can enable *multiple address shipping* as well as limit the number of different addresses to which a customer can ship a single order.

Shipping methods settings

The delivery of products to your customers can be one of the most complex considerations in your business. However, with proper planning and careful attention to details, you can offer your customers affordable shipping methods while keeping your costs reasonable. Shipping and logistics is worthy of its own book!

While we cover table rate shipping in `Chapter 4`, *Preparing to Sell*, we want to take a moment to discuss certain configuration concepts that are common among the various carrier methods provided in a default Magento installation.

Real-time Rates

The carrier-based methods listed in this section (such as **UPS**, **FedEx**, **USPS**, **DHL**, and so on) provide real-time calls to the carrier's computer system to retrieve actual rates for an order based on the weight of the items in the order, the shipping origin and the destination of the shipment. This rate may be more than what you pay, depending on the negotiated rate you have established with a carrier based on your account particulars.

Real-time rates not only provide more accurate shipping rates than fixed or table rates, they also provide a verification of the services that can be provided to the shipping address. For instance, for some addresses, a carrier may not be able to ship overnight, or it may not be able to ship into a certain country.

Test Mode

In most carrier setup configurations, you have the opportunity to use a *test mode* during the setup of your store. As with payment gateways (discussed later in this chapter), testing your configurations is an invaluable way of ensuring that any settings or changes do not adversely affect a live site or send live data to the carrier or gateway. Each carrier has different ways of setting up test or live modes. Refer to their documentation for guidance.

Handling Fee

Most people think of handling fees as additional costs that increase a shopper's shipping expense. Handling fees can either be a percentage or a fixed amount. If you're entering a percentage, enter it as a decimal number. For example, for a 5% handling fee, enter 0.05.

Free Shipping

The creation of free shipping as a shipping option for your customers can be a bit confusing in this panel. The **Free Shipping** method (the first in the list of shipping methods) can be enabled if you want to provide free shipping as an option on each and every order. You can set a minimum order amount, but it is not based on service availability or any carrier restrictions on weight. This method can make it easy to offer a free shipping option across all shipping methods, but only if you're confident you can ship a product to all customers within what you have determined to be an acceptable cost to you.

Within each carrier-based shipping method, there is the opportunity to have Magento provide free shipping opportunities based on a minimum order amount. If you have carrier shipping accounts established, this can be a better way of offering free shipping, as it will only be made available if all conditions for delivery method, destination, and allowed weight are met.

Countries

You should pay careful attention to the countries you choose as available for shipping. If you only ship to addresses within your country, you should select it as the only country in the list of **Ship to Specific Countries** option. By selecting the exact countries into which you will or can ship (your carrier may have restrictions), you are providing customers with clear and professional feedback when they attempt to ship to a country that is not on your approved list. It's better to inform customers upfront, rather than have to contact them after the sale, and deliver the bad news.

Sort Order

As in so many places in Magento, you can control the order in which your shipping methods are displayed to customers by entering a number in this field. Sorting is in ascending order.

Dimensional Weights

Most carriers today calculate shipping rates based on "dimensional weights". Since many packages are light in weight, yet take up as much room as heavier packages, carriers created the concept of dimensional weights to better price for the amount of room that packages take up in their trucks and planes. To calculate your actual weights, carriers multiply the dimensions (width, length, depth) and divide it by a factor (for example, 166). The result of this calculation is compared against the actual weight of the package. Your shipping rate is based on which figure is the greater of the two. Therefore, you might have a package shipping a small, lightweight product in a large box filled with cushioning material that weighs one pound. But, its dimensional weight might be two pounds because of the calculation of the box dimension. Therefore, you would be charged for a two-pound package. You should consult with your carrier to see if your normal packages might be charged at higher rates. If so, you may need to investigate Magento add-ons that can provide you with more accurate shipping rate calculations for your customers.

Google API settings

There's no doubt that Google-and your store's integration with Google services-can have an impact on the traffic to your store.

As with any Google services, if you're not intimately familiar with them, you should seek assistance from others who are. There's a lot of power and opportunity in using these tools; it pays to know how to maximize their features.

Google Analytics

Google provides free traffic analysis tools (`http://www.google.com/analytics/`) that are among the best and most comprehensive in the world. With simple information, Magento embeds the Google Analytics code that captures data about visitors to your site.

- **Enable**: Once you set up your Analytics account, you can activate the code in your Magento store.
- **Account Number**: Enter your **Universal Analytics ID**, which will be in the form "UA-XXXXXXXX-X".

- **Enable Content Experiments**: Google is always working to improve the amount and quality of the data it collects for your analytics account. By enabling this, you're allowing Google and Magento to make adjustments in the underlying code for testing new data-collection techniques.

Google AdWords

If you attract visitors using Google's **pay-per-click** (**PPC**) advertising, you can associate your **AdWords** account with your store so that transactions (that is, conversions) can be tracked against your campaigns, keywords, and ads. Conversions are considered completed checkouts by your customers.

- **Enable**: Set as **Yes** to have Magento add the necessary Google scripting to your pages.
- **Conversion ID**: Enter your Google AdWords conversion ID. You will get this once you have set up conversion tracking in your AdWords account. The ID is a numerical value (that is, no characters).
- **Conversion Language**: Select the language you use in your AdWords account, which may be different from the language of the website.
- **Conversion Format**: Google feels it's important to display a small notice at the bottom of your site telling your visitors that you're collecting analytics data via Google. If you enter a 1 or 2, a small one-line or two-line message will appear respectively. This message will include a **Learn More** link. If you enter 3, no message will appear, but you should add a note in your Privacy Policy that you are using Google Analytics to collect visitor data.
- **Conversion Color**: Enter a hexadecimal color to apply to the Google notice that appears on your site. This only applies if you choose 1 or 2 as the **Conversion Format**.
- **Conversion Label**: The text you enter in this optional field will be used as a label for any conversions that occur on your site.
- **Conversion Value Type**: For most merchants, **Dynamic** is the preferred choice, as it attaches the total of an order as the value of the conversion. You can, however, choose to assign a single, constant value to your conversions.
- **Conversion Value**: Enter the value of any constant conversion type using only numbers and a decimal point. Do not include money prefixes or commas (for example, enter 2000.00 instead of $2,000.00).

Google Shopping

Similar to AdWords, **Google Shopping** allows you to promote your products to Google search users by bidding for placement. Magento 2 can, in conjunction with how you set up your Google Shopping account, feed your products to Google. In Chapter 5, *Products*, we will cover additional settings in your store relating to product preparation for **Google Shopping**.

 Google Shopping is officially called Google Merchants (https://mercha nts.google.com). We're not sure why Magento is retaining this older label, but it is the same.

- **Account ID**: Enter your Google Shopping account ID.
- **Account Login**: Enter your Google account username or e-mail address.
- **Account Password**: Enter your Google account password.
- **Account Type**: You can select your appropriate account type; based on how you configure your Google Shopping account, your feed is either sent to Google (**Google**) or fetched by Google from your Magento server (**Hosted**).
- **Target Country**: Select the target country you specified in your Google account.
- **Update Google Shopping Item when Product is Updated**: Most likely you will want to update Google whenever you make a change to your product.
- **Verifying Meta Tag**: In order to verify your ownership of your store, Google may ask you to add a Meta tag value.
- **Debug:** If you face any difficulty with your product feed, you can turn this on to have debugging information stored to a log on your server. You should probably consult with your developer for assistance.
- **Destinations**: You can choose to provide your product feed for use in multiple Google offerings. Each may have different costs or qualifications. Consult your Google account setup for more information.

Payment Methods settings

Of course, to sell products on your store, you need to provide a means of payment. In Chapter 4, *Preparing to Sell*, we discuss the payment process, as it relates to the checkout process. For our purposes here, we will just go over the different payment methods available to you and how they differ.

The individual processes of configuring, testing, and enabling payment gateways can be rather complex. We strongly suggest consulting with your Magento developer when configuring gateways in order to conduct proper testing, and later, adding the proper credentials for live, secure transactions. Due to the security considerations of payments, you need to make sure that you have SSL encryption, and have taken all proper measures to insure customer data safety.

There are several important decisions you need to make before configuring your payment gateways:

- **Do you want to take credit and debit cards?** If you do, you'll need a **Merchant Account** that allows you to take credit cards.

- **Do you want to allow your customers to enter their credit card information on your site, or would you prefer to allow them to enter the information when they click to place their order?** Taking credit card information on your site adds security issues, such as **PCI compliance** (see the box further in this section).

- **Do you wish to offer subscription type payment services such as PayPal?** According to `BuiltWith.com`, PayPal accounts for about one-third of all online transactions. It's inexpensive and easy to implement, but you do have to have a PayPal business account.

- **Will you allow customers to pay by bank transfer, check, money order, purchase order, or COD?** These methods mean you won't get paid until the customer sends payment or the appropriate paper work. If you're a retailer, you probably won't choose these methods, but if you're a wholesaler, these methods may be quite acceptable.

Whichever payment methods you choose, aim for those that accommodate the type of customers you intend to serve.

The **Payment Card Industry Data Security Standard** (**PCI DSS**), commonly referred to as PCI compliance, means that your website and overall business operation has taken the proper steps to protect customer data. We've all read the headlines over the past few years where major retailers have been hacked, and millions of cardholders' data has been stolen.

If you're taking credit cards online, you should either have your Magento store configured and hosted by a company that provides PCI compliance, or use payment gateways that take credit card information off-site to the payment gateway's website.

One hosting provider we really like is MageMojo (`www.MageMojo.com`), which does provide PCI-compliant hosting servers, especially tuned for Magento stores.

Merchant Location

To begin the configuration process for payments, you need to select your **Merchant Country**. This is usually your home country; it is the one in which you have registered your payment gateway accounts such as PayPal and Authorize.Net.

Braintree

Recently, PayPal boughtBraintree (`www.braintreepayments.com`), a merchant account provider. Many wondered how this acquisition would complement PayPal. Braintree provides additional payment methods to PayPal, such as ApplePay, Venmo, Android Pay, and Bitcoin. Braintree has a pricing model very similar to PayPal Payments (2.9% + 30¢); however, Braintree waives all fees on the first $50,000 of transactions, which can be beneficial if you're a new merchant, and you want a risk-free way of testing Braintree's functionality.

PayPal All-in-One Payment Solutions

While PayPal is no longer a part of the eBay company (which, at the time of this writing, owns Magento), it remains a very visible part of Magento, and for good reason. In our experience, PayPal can offer merchants a complete payment solution including credit and debit cards, e-checks, and credit terms as well as the use of a PayPal account.

The All-in-One solutions refer to the ability to allow your customers to pay by credit card as well as with a PayPal account:

- **Payments Advanced**: Customers are taken to a customized payment portal within PayPal, which reduces your need for PCI compliance.
- **Payments Pro**: You use the credit card form on your Magento site, but the backend processing is performed by PayPal.
- **Payments Standard**: Customers checking out are taken to PayPal to complete their purchase, which they can do with their PayPal account or a credit card. However, it is emphasized that your customers are to use a PayPal account.

With **Payments Advanced** and **Payments Pro**, you set up a Merchant Account with PayPal (as opposed to other merchant account vendors such as FirstData). The fee for transactions is 2.9% plus 30¢ per transaction, and applies to American Express, VISA, MasterCard, and Discover card. Customers who use their PayPal account cost you only a small transaction fee.

PayPal Payment Gateways

If you do have a merchant account, you can still use the convenience and integration of PayPal in your Magento store. **Payflow Pro** uses your Magento credit card checkout process, while **Payflow Link** takes customers to a PCI-compliant web page to complete their purchase. Customers can still use their PayPal account as well.

PayPal Express Checkout

Regardless of whether your use PayPal or another gateway for credit card purchases, you can easily allow customers to use their PayPal account for purchases. PayPal Express can place buy buttons on your product and cart pages to allow shoppers to quickly complete their purchase using a valid PayPal account.

We like using PayPal as it commands a huge portion of the online payment marketplace. When you promote that you use PayPal for your payment processing, it can add credibility to your company. In addition, PayPal takes responsibility for validating customers, and can greatly help with fraud prevention. However, you should seek expert advice when configuring PayPal-as well as any payment method-both in Magento and in your PayPal account, as subtle configurations can make a huge difference on your acceptance policies and your ability to authorize and capture legitimate purchases.

Check/Money Order

Few, if any, online retailers will enable this method, but wholesalers may, particularly where deliveries are not immediately necessary. When you configure this method, you need to provide instructions to customers as to where they should send their payment.

As with any of the available payment methods, you have the ability to edit how the payment method is displayed to customers. The **Title** field in each method can be changed as you wish. For example, instead of **Check / Money Order**, you may want to use `Pay by Cheque` or `Pay by Money Order (no checks allowed)`.

Bank Transfer Payment

Similar to **Check / Money Order**, this is a method that requires a customer to take action after the purchase process. The **Instructions** you provide will be communicated through the customer's order acknowledgement e-mail.

Cash On Delivery Payment

CODs are not as common in online transactions, as merchants rarely have the opportunity to meet or consider the validity of the customer. COD sales require a degree of trust: the merchant trusts that the customer will pay the full amount, including shipping and COD charges when the product is received. If the customer fails to pay or refuses the shipment, the merchant has to pay all the shipping and handling fees, and the sale is not completed.

Zero Subtotal Checkout

In some cases, a transaction may actually end up totaling $0. For example, if you offer a special discount for a free product, and there are no shipping or sales tax charges, the customer may end up with a completely free purchase. You can modify how this situation is communicated to the buyer.

> If a $0 order is possible in your store, you should enable this payment method. Otherwise, the customer will be required to enter credit card or payment information, even if the total is zero.

Purchase Order

Large purchases, particularly in business-to-business transactions, are often created using a purchase order. If you're willing to take purchase orders, you can allow customers to confirm their billing information and enter a PO number for the order.

Authorize.Net Direct Post

If you already have established a payment gateway account with Authorize.Net, you can configure Magento to send your customers to a customizable payment page on the Authorize.Net servers. This is similar to **PayPal Payments Advanced** and **PayPal Payflow Link** in that the sensitive credit card information is captured outside of your Magento server.

Services panels

The Services Panelscontain settings that deal with the interaction of other systems with your Magento store. Due to the complexity and sensitivity of these operations, we suggest you consult with your Magento developer before making any changes to these panels. In all likelihood, you'll have little or no need to edit these settings.

Advanced panels

Much of what exists in the Advanced panels is not relevant to the daily operations of your store, and is more useful to your Magento developer. However, there are a few settings within this section of which you may wish to at least have an understanding. Some deal with security, while others deal with ways to customize your Magento site.

We will touch on those items which we know from experience are more relevant to a store operator. Omitted settings are those for which you should obtain additional assistance from a qualified Magento developer before changing.

Admin settings

Admin User Emails

If you have several people accessing your Magento backend, you will want to provide them with means for recovering forgotten passwords.

- **Forgot Password Email Template**: Select the default or customized e-mail template that will be sent when a backend user requests a forgotten e-mail. The e-mail will contain a link to allow the user to reset their password (actual passwords are not e-mailed to backend users).
- **Forgot and Reset Email Sender**: Select the store contact from which these e-mails should come.
- **Recovery Link Expiration Period (days)**: The link in the e-mail to reset a password expires after a period of time. You can enter the number of days for the expiration.
- **Reset Password Template**: Choose the default or customized e-mail template a user will receive after resetting their password. These e-mails also serve to notify a user that a password change has occurred, in case they did not actually trigger the change.

Startup Page

Select the backend screen you wish users to see after they first log in.

Dashboard

The dashboard shown after login can display charts showing sales activity. These charts take a bit of processing power, so, in some cases, you may wish to turn the charts off.

CAPTCHA

If you fear that login attempts are being made into your backend, you may wish to add a Captcha to the login form as a way to possibly thwart robotic attempts to discover usernames and passwords.

While we didn't directly cover the **Admin Base URL** setting, we do suggest you have your developer configure your system to use a different backend path other than /admin. Since /admin is the default backend path for Magento stores, hackers often work at accessing your store's backend by testing username and password combinations in the login form. If you set your backend path to something other than /admin, hackers will find it much more difficult to discover a way into your store's administration. However, before making any changes to your **Admin Base URL**, consult with your developer, as these changes, if not properly made, could prevent you from logging into your store's backend.

The remaining settings with the **Advanced** panels should only be changed in consultation with your Magento developer. However, we will discuss some of these later in this book, as they pertain to optimization and speed.

Summary

As you can tell, there are many, many possible configurations in your Magento store. People new to Magento may find it quite daunting—I know we did! However, the real power of Magento lies in its ability to be shaped and molded to fit your e-commerce goals.

As we continue through this book, we will revisit some of these settings as we discuss specific business use cases. And as you define your own business operation, you'll return to this chapter over and over again, discovering with each visit that Magento truly is a world-class platform for growing and operating an online store.

There's still lots more to learn-and a lot more configurations ahead-but reading through this chapter and using it as a future reference will help make the following chapters much more useful.

In the next chapter, we continue our configuration tasks by setting up the initial product catalogs and stores. We will begin by doing a bit of planning and understanding the brilliance of the Magento Global-Website-Store methodology.

3
Catalogs and Stores

As we'll explore in this chapter, one of the most powerful features of Magento is demonstrated by the versatility and flexibility of creating a true multi-store environment. Very few e-commerce platforms provide this level of complexity. But what does this mean for you as a store owner?

While you may be just starting out with one online store, chances are that as you grow, you may want to:

- Create additional niche stores
- Sell in multiple languages to a global customer base
- Provide separate storefronts for different users, such as VIP or wholesale customers

While you could create multiple stores on other platforms, Magento uniquely provides the ability to create and manage several web stores within a single backend interface. Each store can appear independent to consumers, but with one login, you-and your staff-can access products, customers, orders, and content across all or any store.

In this chapter, we'll:

- Set up catalogs and categories for group products
- Set up multiple storefronts
- Review various store-specific configurations
- Learn how to manage multiple languages and currencies

We will help you learn and profit from what can be a complex issue by breaking it down into simple steps. First, however, we need to understand how Magento coordinates this hierarchy of websites and storefronts.

The Global-Website-Store methodology

Magento has, since the very beginning of version 1, included a very elegant yet powerful means of creating and configuring multiple stores within a single installation. This structure is based on what we call the **Global-Website-Store** methodology or hierarchy.

Take a look at this diagram:

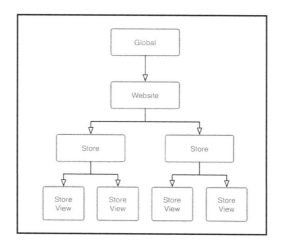

Global refers to any configuration or setting that affects the entire Magento installation. Some settings such as security, product SKUs, and logging apply to all stores.

Website is akin to a business entity as many of the settings made at this level pertain to payment gateways, shipping, taxes, and so on. Therefore, if you have one business entity, you'll most likely have one Website entity, regardless of how many stores you might create within this business. On the other hand, if you want to create another Website entity that has different business-related settings across other stores, Magento makes this possible. In this hierarchy, Website is not the public site your customers visit. Website is the top-level business under which you may have one or more actual web addresses (URLs), each with its own frontend design and content.

 Whenever we use "Website" as a capitalized term, we refer to the Magento Website level or entity. Otherwise, we use "website" in lowercase as the common term for a website viewed in a browser.

Store is the level where you assign a particular product catalog (we'll discuss more on catalogs later). It is at this level that we begin differentiating stores by the products offered. For example, you might have a business called "Acme Inc." with which you want to sell sports apparel and furniture. While "Acme" is the Website entity, you could create separate catalogs for sports apparel and furniture, and create Store entities for each: `AcmeSportswear.com` and `AcmeFurniture.com`, respectively.

It is really only within the Store Configuration aspect of Magento that we see and manipulate Store entities. Throughout the rest of Magento, we will deal with **Store Views**. This is where things get a little confusing, so feel free to reread this section as needed. We think this will become clearer as we work through an example too.

A Store entity can have one or more Store Views. To carry our example further, let's say you want to create English, French, and German versions of `AcmeSportswear.com`. Each of these language sites would constitute a Store View in Magento, all belonging to the one apparel Store entity. Each would have its own domain, such as `AcmeSportswear.com`, `AcmeSportswear.fr`, and `AcmeSportswear.de`.

Throughout Magento, you'll come across a great many settings that can be different for each Store level, such as product descriptions, images, and static content. In fact, the entire design theme for your Store entities can differ by Store View.

While you may only have visions of a single store at present, you'll no doubt find some very creative ways to leverage this multi-store capability to your advantage. With almost any other common platform, you would have to build entire new installations for each language or niche product offerings as well as lose the centralized management of your online "empire."

Creating categories

Before you set out to create your various stores, your first step is to create the necessary categories that represent the products that you will be selling in your Store level. In Magento 2, the *catalog* contains all the products you have in your store. **Categories** are the hierarchal classification of your products and how they will be grouped and represented to your shoppers. Therefore, when we refer to your catalog, we mean the list of products you sell. A product in your catalog can be linked to one or more categories (or none at all).

Each Store entity that you create in Magento 2 must be assigned to one *root category*. Unlike other categories, the root category is never visible to your customers. It is only the topmost category of a Store level; all other categories are *subcategories* of the root category.

Let's think of this association in this manner: a Store level is connected to a root category. A root category is the parent of each top-level product category in your Store entity. As an example, AcmeSportswear.com might be assigned to the *Sportswear* root category (the root category could be any name).

Within the *Sportswear* root category, you might create the first-level categories *Women, Men, Gear, Training, Sale,* and *What's New.* These categories would be the top categories viewed in your store.

When you create the Acme Sportswear Store entity in Magento 2, you would assign it to the *Sportswear* root category.

The categories and products we will use as examples are based on the optional *sample data* provided by Magento during installation. If you're brand new to Magento, you might want to have your developer install the sample data set in order to get a feel for how Magento leverages different types of products, pages, and configurations.

Now that we have an understanding of this relationship, let's create our first root category for Acme Sportswear by going to **Products** > **Categories** in the Magento sidebar menu.

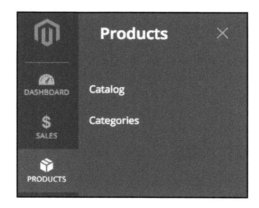

If your Magento 2 is a new installation (with sample data), you should see one default root category called, appropriately, **Default Category**. This category is automatically added during the Magento 2 install, so the default Store entity has a root category with which to be connected.

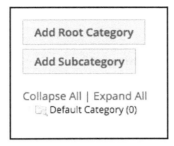

While you can leave the root category named as shown, if you plan to create multiple Store entities with different product categories (more than one Store level can be assigned to the same root category), you might want to rename this default root category to something more meaningful. For our example, let's rename it "Sportswear."

The number in parentheses beside a category name shows the number of products that are assigned to the category and all its subcategories if the **Is Anchor** category setting is set to **Yes**. We'll cover this setting later in this chapter.

1. Click on **Default Category** shown on the left-hand side of the edit area.
2. In the **Name** field, change **Default Category** to **Sportswear**.
3. Click on **Save Category** on the upper right-hand side of the screen (a red button).

You should now see that the name of the top category on the left-hand side has changed.

Now that you have a feel of the category hierarchy, let's create another root category and subcategories for our furniture store:

1. Click on **Add Root Category**.
2. In the **Name** field, enter **Furniture**.
3. Select **Yes** for **Is Active**.
4. Click on **Save Category**.

Creating your category hierarchy

As you work to improve your store, you may want to change your categories and hierarchies. In other cases, your store development process may be in such an early stage that you have little or no idea of what categories you might need. However, let's learn more about creating categories and subcategories.

Let's first build a few top-level categories for our Furniture store, as follows:

1. Click on **Furniture** in the list of categories on the left-hand side, which is the root category we renamed before.

In order to create a subcategory or *nested category*, you have to first select the *parent category*.

2. Click on **Add Subcategory**.
3. For **Name**, enter your first top-level category, such as **Sofas**.

4. To make the category public, select **Yes** for **Is Active**.

5. Click on **Save Category**.

We will go over the remaining fields in this section in just a moment. If you are using this example, your category hierarchy should look similar to this:

You can add more top-level categories, but remember to click on the root category-**Furniture**, in this case-before adding as, by default, Magento selects the category you just added.

Now, let's talk about the other fields and screens within a category detail. These are powerful settings that give you additional flexibility.

The General Information tab

After you saved your first category, you may have noticed that Magento created a value for **URL Key**. This key becomes the path by which you can link directly to the category page in your store. For instance, if the **URL Key** value is **sofas**, you could view the category in your store by going to `yourstore.com/sofas.html` in your browser.

 URL Key values have to be unique within the same level of your category hierarchy. If you use the same URL Key value for more than one category at the same hierarchy level, you will receive an error message.

If you wish to have a description appear at the top of your category page, you can add it in the **Description** field. By clicking on **WYSIWYG Editor**, a larger editing field will appear with additional menu items. As with any *WYSIWYG editor* in Magento, you can add text, images, media, and more.

Adding a good *category description* can help the SEO value of your site by giving search engines more information through which to understand and assess your category page. Your description can also help shoppers better understand what they can expect when perusing the products within. Use this area to promote specials, new brands, and more. This is one of the most overlooked yet beneficial features of managing categories.

For **Image**, you can upload an image related to your category. The position and size of the image shown will depend on your theme.

The next three fields relate specifically to enriching the SEO value of your site. The page title will appear at the top of the browser window as well as in the search results. For example, in the following Google search result, **Beet Harvester Parts** is taken from the **Page Title** value of the category in Magento. The **Tired Iron Tractor Parts** text is automatically added by Magento to all pages (we'll show you how to set this up in Chapter 7, *Content & SEO*).

Beet Harvester Parts - Tired Iron Tractor Parts
www.tiredirontractorparts.com › Home › Agricultural ▾
Replacement parts from Tired Iron are available to replace OEM parts on beet harvesters.

If you don't enter a page title, Magento will automatically use the **Name** category as the page title.

The description that shows in a Google listing is taken from the **Meta Description** value for your category. If you don't enter one, Google will try to create one based on the content of the page. Many times, this results in a description of little or no value to a Google user. Therefore—and, again, we will go into this in more detail in Chapter 7, *Content and SEO* —it's important that you manage your meta descriptions.

If you choose to use meta keywords, you can enter the comma-delimited list in **Meta Keywords**.

Finally, **Include in Navigation Menu** allows you to have a category listed in the *main navigation* on your site.

We're often asked why you would create a category and not have it in the navigation. You may want to create a category of special products, for example, that you wish to show on a web page but not want this groups specifically listed in your navigation menu. With Magento, you can display specific category listings on a page (we'll take a look at an example in `Chapter 7`, *Content & SEO*). This gives you the ability to create unique product groupings without compromising on the primary intent of your main navigation.

Display settings

Magento gives you the ability to customize what is shown on a category page. You may only want to show category pages that contain subcategories but no products. On others, you may want to change how the products are listed.

As you'll learn in `Chapter 7`, *Content and SEO* you can create static blocks, which are sections of content that can be inserted in places on your Store entity's frontend. The *Display mode* can be set to show:

- **Products only**: This displays a list of your products, but no static block is included. If you enter a category description (refer to the preceding section) it will be displayed as well as any category image you include.
- **Static block only**: You can choose a *static block* that you may have created and have it displayed without including a list of products within the category.
- **Static block and products**: This shows a selected static block as well as the products assigned to the category.

The natural question here is, "if I use a category description, why would I build and assign a static block?" Static blocks are often overlooked as a powerful way of creating content that can be assigned to repeated places on your site. For example, let's assume we want to promote a special discount each month throughout your store. If you wanted to have this promo appear on every (or even selected) category pages, you can either manually adjust this content in every category description (which is lots of work), or create a static block that could be edited in one place but assigned to all your categories. We'll cover the creation of static blocks in `Chapter 7`, *Content and SEO*.

As you learn to manage *attributes* in `Chapter 5`, *Products* you'll discover how to create attributes that are *filterable*. Examples of a filterable attribute may be size, color, or price. By filterable, we mean that you can give your customers the ability to narrow their choices in a category list of products by choosing one or more filterable values.

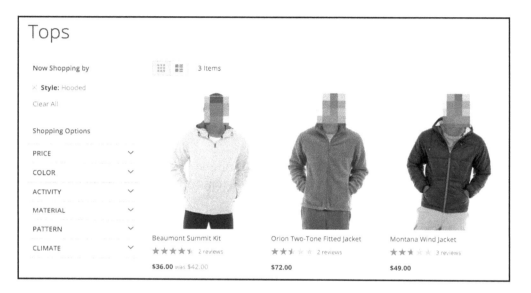

In the preceding screenshot, you can note that within the **Tops** category, we are able to select **Hooded** as a choice for **Style**. This selection filters the products to remove all those that are not configured as **Hooded** garments.

In order to add a **filtered navigation** to your category sidebar, select **Yes** for **Is Anchor** in your **Display Settings** category.

The ability to create complex filtered attributes and use them to help your customers shop more easily is a very powerful Magento feature. The use of attributes, in general, can truly shape your store! So, don't skip the attributes in `Chapter 5`, *Products*.

By default, Magento provides product sorting by **Position**, **Name**, or **Price**. Position refers to the position you choose for the display order of the products (we will discuss this later in this chapter under *Category Products*). In **Available Product Listing Sort By**, you can choose one or more sorting attributes or select **Use All Available Attributes** to include them all.

The next field, **Default Product Listing Sort By**, allows you to select what the default sorting attribute will be.

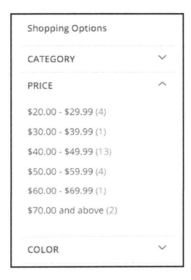

The increments used in building the filtered navigation for price is configurable in your configuration settings (refer to Chapter 2, *Settings and Configurations*). If you wish to use a different *price step*, such as every $5 or every $20, you can enter the number for the step you wish in **Layered Navigation Price Step**, and the price levels shown in the filtered navigation will be adjusted accordingly for the category.

Custom design

An advanced design technique is to create customized layouts for use in specific situations. For example, you may want a completely different category layout for a category of downloadable products, or you may wish to simply change the number of columns displayed for a particular category.

- **Use Parent Category Settings**: If you wish to have a category *inherit* its design settings from its parent category, set this to **Yes**.
- **Apply to Products**: You can also choose to apply any special layout changes of the parent category to the products displayed within a selected category.
- **Custom Design**: Your developer can set up alternative themes that you can assign to a particular category. The alternative theme could contain a category layout with different positioning, branding, and more.

- **Active From and Active To**: If you do choose an alternative theme, you can also choose the dates from which and to which the alternative theme will be applied. This can be useful, for instance, if you have a theme constructed specifically for a holiday season.
- **Page Layout**: For a category (and any subcategories that you choose **Use Parent Category Settings** for), you can alter the default theme layout for categories by choosing an alternative layout, such as one column, two columns with a left-hand side bar, and so on.
- **Custom Layout Update**: Your developer can also alter a category's layout by constructing XML code that affects how a page is rendered in Magento. If so, this XML code is inserted into this field.

Category products

In most cases, you will assign products to categories as you build the products in Magento. However, you can also assign products and adjust their *position* in this panel.

You can search for products in your store and assign them to the category by selecting the box in the far left-hand side of each row.

 By default, this panel displays all the assigned products—those that are already checked. To search for other products that are not already assigned, be sure to change the first column heading of the drop-down menu to **No** or **Any**.

If you choose to manage the order in which your products are displayed in a category listing (refer to the **Display Settings** section shown earlier), you can enter a number in the **Position** column. You can enter any number knowing that the default sort order is ascending or lower number first. Therefore, if you want to order products, you would enter the lowest number for the first product you wish to display and then go up from there (for example, 1, 2, 3 or 10, 20, 30). You can use any sequence of numbers. Any having the same number will be sorted by **ID** (the second column), which is the product's internal Magento record number.

Now that you have your categories established, it's time to turn to setting up your stores.

Creating Website and Store entities

Most store owners who use Magento for the first time will have only one store. In fact, it's quite natural to "get your feet wet" by learning the full power and extent of Magento by building and managing a single Store entity. However, as we pointed out, there can be tremendous power in leveraging Magento's ability to operate multiple stores within a single backend.

 You can contrast Magento's multistore capability with other lesser platforms, in which you have to build each store individually. In these cases, you would have to log into each individual backend to manage your products, orders, and customers. Furthermore, selling the same inventory across multiple stores becomes a considerable synchronization challenge.

Let's begin by revisiting our example Global-Website-Store hierarchy:

- We want to create two Store entities for sportswear and furniture: www.AcmeSportswear.com and www.AcmeFurniture.com, respectively
- For the sportswear website, we want to create three Store Views in English, French, and German: www.AcmeSportswear.com, www.AcmeSportswear.fr and www.AcmeSportswear.de, respectively

 Please note that the creation of multiple URLs for multiple stores may require some configuration by your developer: be sure to consult with your developer to ensure that your stores are properly accessible.

The first decision, based on our example, is whether you want to set up separate Website entities for each Store one. As certain Magento configurations can be changed only at the Website level, it's important to consider whether your hierarchy will be as follows:

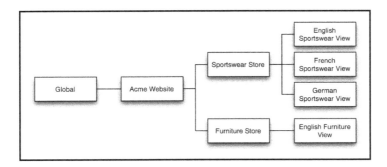

Alternatively, it could be a multiple website hierarchy, such as the following:

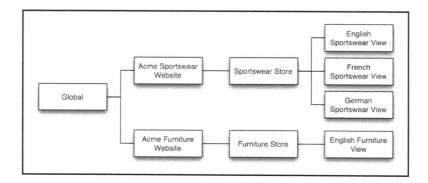

It's also possible—and conceivably, logical—to even choose a hierarchy such as the following:

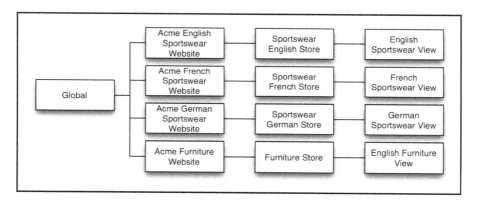

While the difference may appear subtle—and there are even more ways to construct the same entities—there are implications and reasons of choosing one hierarchy scheme over another. Generally, the choice comes down to control and flexibility. Based on your business objectives, you may need more flexibility in terms of how you configure the different backend settings such as payments, shipping, and inventory. At the same time, you need to decide how you wish to use products across multiple stores. Pricing and currency conversions can also play a big role in how you choose your setup.

We highly suggest that you have your developer set up a development or test Magento installation for you to use to take a look at which hierarchy will work best for your purposes. The time you take to consider different configurations will be more than outweighed by the benefits of setting up your stores correctly. It's okay if you're not ready to consider multiple stores: set up a simple, one-level store configuration for now. You'll be able to wisely add more Website and Store entities to your installation as you gain experience with Magento.

In our example, we will choose the second hierarchy displayed earlier based on our hypothetical business objectives:

- We want to set up sportswear and furniture as their own business units, each with their own product catalog, inventory, and other configurations
- We still want the ability to provide global configurations across all stores, but payments will go into separate accounts for each business unit
- We're okay with using automatic currency conversions for the different language stores based on the default price and currency for products

If you want to manually set prices for products in different currencies—that is, not use an automatic currency conversion—you would need to use something similar to the third flow chart shown in the preceding figures. Prices can only be set globally or per website but not at the Store View level.

Creating Websites

Let's begin by going to **Stores** | **All Stores** in your backend menu.

The preceding is the default that will appear with any new Magento installation. To set up our two websites, let's start by renaming **Main Website**, which is the default:

1. Click on **Main Website**.
2. Change the **Name** parameter to `Sportswear Website`.
3. If you wish, you can also change Code to any lowercase word (with no spaces), such as "sportswear."

If you're working on a live production store installation (and you shouldn't!), you may need to ask your developer whether changing the Code will have any adverse effects. Some developers use this code in the `index.php` file (however, we don't advocate this methodology).

4. Click on **Save Web Site**.

Next, let's create Furniture Website:

1. Click on **Create Website**.
2. Enter `Furniture Website` for **Name**.
3. Enter `furniture` for **Code**.
4. Then, click on **Save Web Site**.

Your Stores panel should now look similar to this:

You'll notice that **Furniture Website** has no **Store** entity or **Store View**, and **Sportswear Website** only has the one, the default Store. Let's fix this now.

If you want to display your Website and Store entities in a different order other than alphabetical, and you can enter a number in the **Sort Order** field of each.

Creating Store entities

Let's start with Furniture Website:

1. Click on **Create Store** at the top of the screen.
2. Make sure that **Furniture Website** is chosen in the **Web Site** drop-down menu.
3. Enter `Furniture Store` for **Name** (you can use any name you wish).
4. Choose **Furniture** for **Root Category** to assign the product catalog containing your furniture products to this Store entity.
5. Click on **Save Store**.

Now, let's rename the Sportswear Website Store entity:

1. Click on the **Main Website Store** link in the Stores panel.
2. Change the **Name** parameter to "Sportswear Store."
3. Click on **Save Store**.

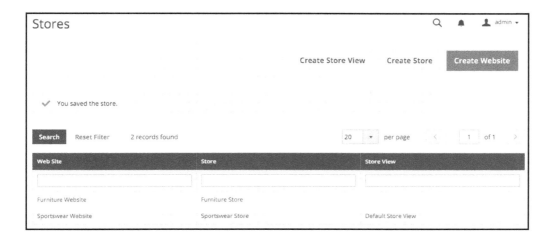

You're almost there! The next step is to create the various Store Views that will ultimately dictate what your customers will see as they visit your online stores.

Creating Store Views

Again, let's begin with the one Furniture Store View we need:

1. Click on **Create Store View** at the top of the Stores panel screen.
2. Select **Furniture Store** for **Store**.
3. Enter **Furniture English View** for **Name** (you can use whatever name you wish).
4. Enter a lowercase **Code**. You can use underscores ("_"), as well, but no spaces or other characters than letters and numbers.

> We often use a language abbreviation in **Code**, such as `furniture_en` for Furniture, English. You can, of course, use `furniture_english`, or if you're not going to create multiple languages, simply use `furniture` or `furniture_store`.

5. Select **Enabled** for **Status** unless you don't want the Store View active for any reason.
6. Click on **Save Store View**.

To create the first Store View for the Sportswear Store entity, perform the following steps:

1. Click on **Default Store View**, as shown in the list of Stores.
2. Update the **Name** parameter to something similar to Sportswear English View.
3. You can leave **Code** as the default, but for consistency's sake, you may want to change it to `sportswear_en` or similar.
4. Click on **Save Store View**.

 As with Website Code, consult with your developer if you're working on a live Magento installation before changing.

 The Store View code may appear in your store URLs (for example, `www.AcmeSportswear.com/sportswear_en/apparel.html`) based on your configurations (refer to `Chapter 2`, *Settings and Configurations*). If so, you may want to take care with what you choose as the Store View code.

To create additional Sportswear Store Views, use the same technique you used to create the Furniture English Store View, substituting the appropriate language nomenclature where appropriate (for example, `sportswear_fr` and `sportswear_de` for the French and German sites, respectively).

When completed, your Stores panel should look similar to:

Web Site	Store	Store View
Furniture Website	Furniture Store	Furniture English View
Sportswear Website	Sportswear Store	Sportswear English View
Sportswear Website	Sportswear Store	Sportswear French View
Sportswear Website	Sportswear Store	Sportswear German View

The frontend selector

Once you set up multiple Store Views for a site, you'll notice that on your store frontend, a selector may appear that allows customers to select an alternative view. The availability and position of this selector is theme-dependent and may be removed or hidden if necessary (consult with your Magento developer for assistance).

If you want the Store Views to display different names than show, simply change the **Name** field of the Store View in your Stores panel.

Configuring Store information

Now that you have created multiple Website and Store entities and Store Views, it's important to review your configuration settings as they pertain to how you wish to communicate information among the different stores.

This is also a good opportunity to learn how to manage your multiple stores within the Magento interface.

Understanding the Configuration Scope

When you go to **Stores** | **Configuration**, you will notice a new drop-down menu at the upper left-hand side of the screen.

This menu—that is, **Store View**—allows you to select the **Configuration Scope** of your configuration settings. That is, if you wish to manage configurations only for **Sportswear French View**, you would select this view in the drop-down menu.

 As you work with configuration settings, it is very important that you pay attention to your Scope choice. Choosing the incorrect Scope can have effects beyond what you expect.

When working at various Scope levels, keep in mind:

- Not all configurations are available at all Scopes. For instance, you can only set Payment Gateway at the Website level, although you can make some choices regarding language and currency at the Store View level.
- You cannot choose a Store entity as Configuration Scope; only Website and Store View can be chosen. Therefore, if you want different Website level settings for different Store Views, you have to create multiple Website entities for each Store View.
- Configurations at the lowest Configuration Scope will supersede configurations at higher levels. For example, if you make a selection at the Store View level, it will override a selection made at the Website or Default Config level.

- The "Default Config" level configures Global settings. Most—but not all—can be overridden at the Website and/or Store View levels.
- As you go through various configurations, the lowest possible Configuration Scope for a given setting will be shown to the right in brackets ("[]").

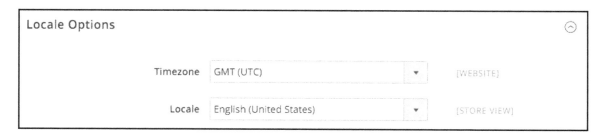

In the preceding screen shot, **Timezone** can only be changed at the Website Configuration Scope, whereas **Locale** is configurable at each Store View.

Remember that when we discuss changing the "Scope," we're usually asking you to make a selection in the **Store View** drop-down menu at the top of any backend panel.

Configuring Store settings

While you should review all the configuration settings after modifying your Stores, you should particularly pay attention to the following:

- Update store addresses and contact information.
- Configure any specific URLs for stores, such as `www.AcmeSportswear.fr` or `www.AcmeSportswear.de`. You may need assistance from your Magento developer to configure your server to honor these domains and cause them to render the appropriate Store View to your customers.
- Review the transactional e-mails and create new templates, if necessary, to reflect different store policies, hours, and so on. (refer to `Chapter 8`, *Promotions and Communications*).
- Modify titles and names as needed for various languages. For instance, you may want to change how "Credit/Debit Card" is displayed based on the language of the site.

- Start your configurations at the Default Config level and work downwards. That is, review each configuration at the top Configuration Scope, and as you determine that you may need to make changes at lower levels, switch your Configuration Scope and make the appropriate change. In this way, you'll have the fewest modifications to make and track.

Accommodating multiple languages

The versatility of multiple Store Views comes into real power as you configure your stores for various languages (and currencies, which are explained later in this chapter). To truly provide a native language experience for your customers, you have to:

- Assign a locale to a store.
- Update configurations where applicable for the appointed language.
- Translate categories and products where necessary.
- Translate other site content.

For this exercise, let's focus on the French Sportswear website.

Assigning a locale

To begin, go to **Stores** | **Configuration** and click on the **General** panel within the **General** side menu.

Select **Sportswear French View** in the upper-left **Store View** drop-down menu. This changes the Configuration Scope so that you can make changes that only affect this Store View.

Expand the **Locale Options** panel.

You'll notice that **Use Website** is selected beside each field. This means that by default, each setting inherits its configuration from whatever is configured at the Website Configuration Scope level. It's also quite possible that the settings at the Website level are set to inherit from the Default Config level, but for this, we're only concerned with modifying the Store View settings.

Therefore, to change a setting at this Configuration Scope level, simply unselect the **Use Website** box. The field will then become editable.

1. Unselect the **Use Website** box to the right of the **Locale** field.
2. Select **French (France)** in the **Locale** drop-down menu.
3. Click on **Save Config**.

Depending on your theme, when switching to the French Store View, you will notice changes in some of the copy on the site.

Note that not all items on a site will be translated. Read on for directions on how to change the items that are not changed by your language choice.

Updating configurations

As mentioned earlier, you may need to review how various features are titled based on the chosen language. As an example, let's look at how a payment method might be displayed to your customer.

Leave your Configuration Scope set to **Sportswear French View** and go to the **Sales │ Payment Methods** panel. Expand the **Check / Money Order** panel. You'll notice that, by default, the Title is **Check / Money Order**. Let's change this to French as **Chèque / Mandat Postal**.

1. Unselect the **Use Website** box.
2. Change **Title** to **Chèque / Mandat Postal**.
3. Click on **Save Config**.

Now, if you have this payment method enabled (which can only be done at the Website Configuration Scope level), your customers visiting www.AcmeSportswear.fr would see **Chèque / Mandat Postal** as the title for paying by check or money order.

You can see now that not only can you update titles by language, but you can also change the title itself! You may, in this case, decide that you only want to use the word "Check" in the English view or use "Company Check Only." Magento gives you tremendous flexibility to customize your stores as you like.

Translating products and categories

As with configuration settings, you can also update products and categories in a similar fashion by editing categories and products at the appropriate Configuration Scope. As an example, let's take another look at our sample default store theme in the French view.

Note that the names of the categories at the top are all in English! How *inapproprié*!

To change the name of the Women category name, for example, select this category in your Magento backend under **Products | Categories**. Choose **Sportswear French View** in the **Store View** Configuration Scope menu to the upper-left.

For Name, enter `Femmes` and click on **Save Category**. Now when viewing the frontend, you'll see that Women is changed to Femmes in the top navigation bar.

Easy, *oui*?

It's tempting, we know, to consider using a translation *engine* that will automatically translate your site on the fly, so to speak. If you've ever translated a foreign language site using Google or some other mechanism, you know first-hand that computed translations often misinterpret content because they don't understand context. Furthermore, the translation may not convey the sense of what was intended in terms of tone or passion. If you are building stores in multiple languages, you should take the time and effort to translate your content manually. Don't insult your foreign audiences: speak to them as you would speak to someone in your own language. There are lots of qualified translators available through such sites as Upwork (`www.upwork.com`). You might also consider hiring a local college student who has native speaking and writing skills in your desired language.

Translating other content

In Chapter 7, *Content and SEO* we will discuss creating static content for your site, such as the About Us page or your Privacy Policy page. As with configurations, products, and categories, you can create **CMS** content that will only show for certain Store Views. We'll show you how in Chapter 7,*Content and SEO*.

However, not all content is easily accessible for translation. For example, if you look closely at the previous screen shot, you'll notice the link for **Sign In** at the very top of the screen. This is a link that takes a customer to a login form where they can log in to your store and retrieve order information, update their addresses, and more.

There are basically two ways to change this from "Sign In" to "Se Connecter" for your French language store (you might choose some other French word; we're using *se connecter* for our example).

The first way uses a *translation file*. This is a text file stored on your Magento server that lists each default phrase paired with a translated substitute. These are often automatically used when you change the **Locale** setting, as we did earlier. For these to work, a translation file for your desired locale must be present on the server.

In our example, a translation file for French is not present on our installation. Otherwise, Sign In would have already shown a French equivalent. If you want to use a translation file—or alter what is used as translations—you should have your Magento developer provide the file for you to review or change. Then, they can install it on your server.

The second means of translating labels and other such content is using the Inline Translation feature of Magento. This is a very powerful tool to translate your storefront as you find necessary.

To change Sign In on our example store, perform the following steps:

1. Go to the **Advanced | Developer** panel under **Stores | Configuration**.
2. Change **Store View** at the top to "Sportswear French View."
3. Expand the **Translate Inline** panel.
4. Unselect the **Use Website** box to the right of the **Enabled for Storefront** field.
5. Select **Yes** for the field.
6. Click on **Save Config**.
7. Clear your cache if necessary by going to **System | Cache Management** and clicking on **Flush Magento Cache**.
8. Refresh your home page. You should now see red borders around any translatable content.

9. Hover your mouse over Sign In and a small *book* icon will appear. Click on this icon to create a pop-up window.

In this box, you can change the **Translated** value for your selection. As you can see in this example, the translated value for Sign In is the same as the original value. This is because there is no French translation file for this particular theme. That's okay as we can change the value by entering `Se Connecter` in the **Custom** field.

If you want this translation to only take effect for the particular Store View you're viewing (French, in this case), select the **Store View Specific** checkbox. Otherwise, the value you enter will affect all your Stores. Click on **Soumettre** (French for "submit"; this is in French because of our Locale setting) to save your changes.

Flush your Magento cache in the backend and refresh your page. You should now see the following:

When you're finished translating, be sure to set **Enabled for Storefront** in the **Translate Inline** panel back to **No** or select the **Use Website** box and click on **Save Config**.

Configuring multiple currencies

In most cases where you're building stores for multiples languages or if you simply want to offer customers greater convenience, you can set Magento to provide pricing in *multiple currencies*. For this exercise, we will combine both possibilities:

- We will offer prices on the English sportswear site in US Dollars and Euros.
- We will display prices on the French and German sportswear sites in Euros as well as British Pound Sterling, Japanese Yen, and US Dollars.

As all these sites are Store entities within the same Website entity, we can't manually set prices at different currencies, but we will set Magento to calculate the different prices based on the periodically updated *currency conversion rates*.

 Remember that manually offering different prices on the same product requires multiple Website entities, each connected to the same catalog. You also would need to navigate to **Catalog Price Scope** in **Stores** | **Configuration** | **Catalog** | **Price** and set it to **Website**.

Setting up currencies

For each Website (for example, Sportswear and Furniture) entity, regardless of the currencies offered in the Store Views, you have to designate the currency with which you will manage product prices. For instance, in the Sportswear Website, you may choose to manage prices in US Dollars even though dollars will not be used for the French and German store views. Conversely, you could also choose to manage prices as Euros, whereas the English site only shows prices in dollars and pounds.

Therefore, the first step is to designate the currency of your Website entity—in this case, Sportswear Website. Perform the following:

1. Go to the **Currency Setup** panel in **Stores** | **Configuration** | **General**.
2. Change your **Store View** Configuration Scope to Sportswear Website.
3. If you need to change **Default Display Currency**, unselect the **Use Default** checkbox, choose your preference, and click on **Save Config**.

Once you're pleased with your choice, change **Store View** to Sportswear French View so that you can set the currencies for this Store View. Following our exercise, perform these steps:

1. Go to **Stores** | **Configuration** | **Currency Setup**.
2. Select **Sportswear French View** in the **Store View** drop-down menu.
3. In the center section, select **British Pound Sterling, Euro, Japanese Yen**, and **US Dollar** in the **Allowed Currencies** selection field (we're adding a couple of extra ones for illustrative purposes).
4. Select **Euro** in the **Default Display Currency** drop-down menu.
5. Click on **Save Config**.

To set up the German site, perform exactly the same steps as you did for the French site.

Configuring currency conversions

Now that you have the currencies set up in your store, it's time to configure Magento to automatically update the currency conversion rates that will be used to translate US Dollars into British Pounds Sterling, Canadian Dollars, and Euros. Magento uses a public service called **Webservicex** to keep your currency conversions up to date. Perform the following steps:

Go to **Stores** | **Currency Rates**.

As you can note, there is one row based on the fact that we only set US Dollars as the **Base Currency** for Sportswear Website. If we set another Website entity at another base currency, we would see another row for this currency as well. In this example, other currencies will be calculated compared to $1 USD.

The Euro conversion factor is already showing because we set the French and German Store Views to use Euro as **Default Display Currency**.

To generate conversion factors for the other currencies we chose, click on **Import**.

Once imported, the new conversion factors are shown for their respective currencies. In addition, the previous factor is shown below any new rate that changed (refer to **Old rate** in the preceding image). Be sure to click on **Save Currency Rates** once you're satisfied with the import.

Now, when you view the store on the frontend, you'll see a drop-down menu allowing your customer to display prices in various currencies.

Once you have your initial currency rates established, you need to configure Magento to retrieve currency updates automatically.

 If you want to manually manage currency rates instead of having Magento automatically update the various conversion factors, you can choose to forego the following configuration. However, you will be subject to possible losses due to currency fluctuations.

1. Go to **Stores** | **Configuration** | **General** | **Currency Setup** in the backend.
2. Expand the **Scheduled Import Settings** panel.
3. If you wish to enable the automatic updates, select **Yes** for **Enabled**.
4. You can also select the time each day you wish to have the system update the conversion factors as well as the frequency (daily, weekly, or monthly).
5. Enter an e-mail address if you wish to receive a notification if the update fails. If you suspect wide currency fluctuations, it may be important to know if a currency update fails.
6. Click on **Save Config**.

Summary

We can't compliment Magento enough for building a great mechanism to manage multiple Website and Store entities within a single installation. This one feature alone can truly make your store ownership experience more powerful and more enjoyable.

You also have the power to create multiple language sites and give customers the convenience of purchasing in currencies they find more familiar. With Magento, you can truly build a global online e-commerce machine.

In Chapter 4, *Preparing to Sell* we will continue the process of configuring our stores for business by covering items related to the financial and shipping aspects of your store.

Indeed, setting up an online store for profitable selling is complex. However, it is also rewarding once your Magento is configured to find that everything is humming along and customers are cheerfully buying your products or services.

4
Preparing to Sell

So far, you've come a long way toward opening and operating a viable online store; however, e-commerce doesn't work unless customers actually purchase a product or service. In order to make that happen on your Magento store, you need to take payments, provide shipping solutions, collect any required taxes, and, of course, process orders.

In this chapter, we're going to:

- Understand the checkout and payment process
- Discuss various payment methods you can offer your customers
- Configure table rate shipping and review other shipping options
- Explore the use of **Customer Groups**
- Learn how to create and manage tax rates and rules
- Explain how to manage the order process

It's extremely important that you take care to understand and manage these aspects of your online business, as this involves money – the customer's and yours. No matter how great your products or your pricing, if customers cannot purchase easily, understand your shipping and delivery, or feel in the least hesitant about completing their transaction, your customer leaves, and neither they nor you achieve satisfactory results. Once an order is placed you also have to take steps to process the purchase and make good on your obligation of fulfilling your customer's request.

Fortunately-like many other aspects of online commerce, Magento has the features and tools required to create a solid, efficient checkout experience.

Understanding the checkout and payment process

Since most people shopping online today have made at least one e-commerce purchase through a website, the general process of completing an order is fairly well-established, although the exact steps will vary somewhat:

1. Customer reviews their shopping cart, confirming the items they have decided to purchase.
2. Customer enters their shipping destination information.
3. Customer chooses a shipping method based on cost, method, and time of delivery.
4. Customer enters their payment information.
5. Customer reviews their order, and confirms their intent to purchase.
6. The system (Magento, in our case) queries a payment processor for approval.
7. The order is completed and ready for processing.

Of course, as we'll explore in this chapter, you'll see there is much more detail related to this process. As online merchants, you would want your customers to have a thorough, yet easy, purchasing experience, and you would want a valid order that can be fulfilled without complications.

To achieve both ends, you have to prepare your Magento store to accurately process orders. So, let's jump in.

Payment methods

When a customer places an order on your Magento store, you'll naturally want to provide a means of capturing payment, whether it's immediate (credit card, PayPal, and the like) or delayed (COD, check, money order, or credit). Of course, the *payment methods* you choose to provide are up to you, but you'll want to provide methods that reduce your risk of not getting paid, as well as provide convenience to your customers while fulfilling their payment expectations. Consumers expect to pay by credit card or through a third-party service such as PayPal. Wholesale buyers may expect to purchase using a **Purchase Order**, or by sending you a check before shipment. As with any business, you have to decide what will best benefit both you and your buyers.

How payment gateways work

If you're new to online payments as a merchant, it's helpful to have an understanding of how payments are approved and captured in e-commerce. For this explanation, we're focusing on those *payment gateways* that allow you to accept credit and debit cards in your store. While **PayPal Express** and **PayPal Standard** work in a similar fashion, the three gateways that are included in the default Magento installation, **PayPal Payments**, **Braintree**, and **Authorize.Net**, process credit and debit cards similarly. The process is described as follows:

1. Your customer enters their card information in your website during checkout.
2. When the order is submitted, Magento sends a request to the gateway (PayPal Payments, Braintree, or Authorize.net) for authorization of the card.
3. The gateway submits the card information and order amount to a clearing house service that determines if the card is valid, and the order amount does not exceed the credit limit of the cardholder.
4. A success or failure code is returned to the gateway and on to the Magento store. If the intent is to capture the funds at the time of purchase, the gateway will queue the capture into a batch for processing later in the day, and notify Magento that the funds are *captured*.
5. A successful transaction will commit the order in Magento, and a failure will result in a message to the purchaser.

Other payment methods, such as PayPal Standard and PayPal Express, take the customer to the payment provider's website to complete the payment portion of the transaction. Once the payment is completed, the customer is returned to your Magento store front.

When properly configured, integrated payment gateways will update Magento orders as they are authorized and/or captured. This automation means you spend less time managing orders and more time fulfilling shipments and satisfying your customers!

PCI compliance

The protection of your customer's payment information is extremely important. Not only would a breach of security cause damage to your customer's credit and financial accounts, but the publicity of such a breach could be devastating to your business.

Merchant account providers will require that your store meet stringent guidelines for PCI compliance, a set of security requirements called PCI DSS. Your ability to be PCI-compliant is based on the integrity of your hosting environment, and by what methods you allow customers to enter credit card information on your site.

Magento 2 no longer offers a Stored Credit Card payment method. It is highly unlikely that you could, or would want to, provide a server configuration secure enough to meet PCI DSS requirements for storing credit card information. You probably don't want the liability exposure as well.

You can, however, provide **SSL Encryption** that could satisfy PCI compliance as long as the credit card information is encrypted before being sent to your server, and then from your server to the credit card processor. As long as you're not storing the customer's credit card information on your server, you can meet PCI compliance if your hosting provider can assure compliance for server and database security.

 Even with SSL encryption, not all hosting environments will pass PCI DSS standards. It's vital that you work with a hosting company that has real Magento experience, and can document proof of PCI compliance.

Therefore, you should decide whether to provide onsite or offsite credit card payments. In other words, do you want to take payment information within your Magento checkout page, or redirect the user to a payment service, such as PayPal, to complete their transaction?

There are pros and cons of each method. Onsite transactions may be perceived as less secure, and you do have to prove PCI compliance to your merchant account provider on an ongoing basis. However, onsite transactions mean that the customer can complete their transaction without leaving your website. This helps to preserve your brand experience for your customers.

Fortunately, Magento is versatile enough to allow you to provide both options to your customers. Personally, we feel that offering multiple payment methods means you're more likely to complete a sale, while also showing your customers that you want to provide the most convenience in purchasing.

Let's now review the various payment methods offered by default in Magento 2.

 Magento 2 comes with a host of the most popular and common payment methods. However, you should review other possibilities, such as **Amazon Payments**, **Stripe**, and **Moneybookers**, depending on your target market. We anticipate that developers will be offering add-ons for these and other payment methods.

 Note that as you change the **Merchant Location** at the top of the **Payment Methods** panel, the payment methods available to you may change.

PayPal all-in-one payment solutions

While PayPal is commonly known for their quick and easy PayPal Express buttons, the ubiquitous yellow buttons you see throughout the web, PayPal can provide you with credit/debit card solutions that allow customers to use their cards without needing a PayPal account. To your customer, the checkout appears no different than if they were using a normal credit card checkout process.

The big difference is that you have to set up a business account with PayPal before you can begin accepting non-PayPal account payments. Proceeds will go almost immediately into your PayPal account (you have to have a PayPal account), but your customers can pay by using a credit/debit card or their own PayPal account.

With the All-in-One solution available in certain countries, PayPal approves your application for a merchant account and allows you to accept all popular cards, including American Express, at a flat 2.9% rate, plus $0.30/transaction. PayPal payments incur normal per transaction PayPal charges.

 We like this solution, as it keeps all your online receipts in one account, while also giving you fast access to your sales income. PayPal also provides a debit card for its merchants that can earn back 1% on purchases. We use our PayPal debit card for all kinds of business purchases, and receive a nice little cash-back dividend each month.

PayPal provides two ways to incorporate credit card payment capture on your website:

- **PayPal Payments Advanced**: Inserts a form on your site that is actually hosted from PayPal's highly secure servers. The form appears as part of your store, but you don't have any PCI compliance concerns.

- **PayPal Payments Pro**: Allows you to obtain payment information using the normal Magento form, and then submit it to PayPal for approval.

The difference to your customer is that with Advanced, there is a slight delay while the credit card form is inserted into the checkout page. You may also have some limitations in terms of styling.

PayPal Payments Standard, also a part of the All-in-One solution, takes your customer to a PayPal site for payment. Unlike PayPal Express, however, you can style this page to better reflect your brand image. Plus, customers do not have to have a PayPal account in order to use this checkout method.

PayPal payment gateways

If you already have a merchant account for collecting online payments, you can still utilize the integration of PayPal and Magento by setting up a PayPal business account that is linked to your merchant account. Instead of paying PayPal a percentage of each transaction (you would pay this to your merchant account provider) you simply pay a small per transaction fee.

PayPal Express

Offering PayPal Express is as easy as having a PayPal account. It does require some configuration of API credentials, but it does provide the simplest means of offering payment services without setting up a merchant account.

PayPal Express will add **Buy Now** buttons to your product pages and the cart page of your store, giving shoppers a quick and immediate ability to checkout using their PayPal account.

Braintree

PayPal recently acquired Braintree, a payment services company that adds additional services to merchants. While many of their offerings appear to overlap PayPal's, Braintree brings additional features to the marketplace such as **Bitcoin**, **Venmo**, **Android Pay**, and **Apple Pay** payment methods apart from **recurring billing,** and **fraud protection**. Like PayPal Payments, Braintree charges 2.9% + $0.30/transaction.

A Word about Merchant Fees
While operating our own e-commerce businesses for many years, we have used many different merchant accounts and gateways. At first glance, 2.9%, offered by PayPal, Braintree, and Stripe, appear to be expensive percentages. If you've been solicited by merchant account providers, you no doubt have been quoted rates as low as 1.7%. What is not often disclosed is that this rate only applies to basic cards that do not contain miles or other premiums. Rates for most cards you accept can be quite high. American Express usually charges more than 3% on transactions. Once you factor in gateway costs, reporting, monthly account costs, and so on, you may find, as we did, that our total merchant costs using a traditional merchant account averaged over 3.3%! One cost you may not think to factor is the expense of setup and integration. PayPal and Braintree have worked hard to create easy integration with Magento (Stripe is not yet available for Magento 2 as of this writing).

Check / money order

If you have customers for whom you will accept payment by check and/or money order, you can enable this payment method. Be sure to enter all the information fields, especially **Make Check Payable to** and **Send Check to**. You will most likely want to keep the **New Order Status** as **Pending**, which means the order is not ready for fulfillment until you receive payment and update the order as Paid.

As with any payment method, be sure to edit the **Title** of the method to reflect how you wish to communicate it to your customers. If you only wish to accept money orders, for instance, you might change the **Title** to `Money Orders (sorry, no checks).`

Bank transfer payment

As with check / money order, you can allow customers to wire money to your account by providing information to your customers who choose this method.

Cash On Delivery payment

Likewise, you can offer COD payments. We still see this method being made available on wholesale shipments, but very rarely on **business-to-consumer** (B2C) sales. COD shipments usually cost more, so you will need to accommodate this added fee in your pricing or shipping methods. At present, there is no ability to add a COD fee using this payment method panel.

Zero subtotal checkout

If your customer, by use of discounts or credits, or selecting free items, owes nothing at checkout, enabling this method will cause Magento to hide payment methods during checkout. The content in the **Title** field will be displayed in these cases.

Purchase order

In **business-to-business** (B2B) sales, it's quite common to accept **purchase orders** (POs) for customers with approved credit. If you enable this payment method, an additional field is presented to customers for entering their PO number when ordering.

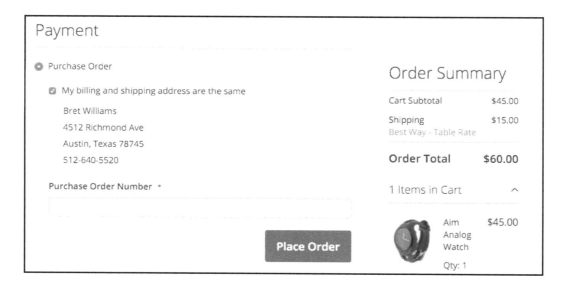

Authorize.Net Direct Post

Authorize.Net, perhaps the largest payment gateway provider in the USA, provides an integrated payment capture mechanism that gives your customers the convenience of entering credit/debit card information on your site, but the actual form submission bypasses your server and goes directly to Authorize.Net. This mechanism, as with PayPal Payments Advanced, lessens your responsibility for PCI compliance as the data is communicated directly between your customer and Authorize.Net instead of passing through the Magento programming.

 In Magento 1.x, the regular Authorize.Net gateway **Advanced Integration Method** (**AIM**) was one of several default payment methods. We're not certain it will be added as a default in Magento 2, although we would imagine someone will build an extension. Regardless, we think Direct Post is a wonderful way to use Authorize.Net, and meet your PCI compliance obligations.

Shipping methods

Once you get paid for a sale, you need to fulfill the order, and that means you have to ship the items purchased. *How* you ship products is largely a function of what shipping methods you make available to your customers.

Shipping is one of the most complex aspects of e-commerce, and one where you can lose money if you're not careful. As you work through your shipping configurations, it's important to keep the following things in mind:

- What you charge your customers for shipping does not have to be exactly what you're charged by your carriers. Just as you can offer free shipping, you can also charge flat rates based on weight or quantity, or add a surcharge to *live* rates.
- By default, Magento does not provide you with highly sophisticated shipping rate calculations, especially when it comes to *dimensional* shipping. Consider shipping rate calculations as *estimates* only. Consult whoever is actually doing your shipping to determine if any rate adjustments should be made to accommodate dimensional shipping.

Dimensional shipping refers to a recent change by UPS, FedEx, and others to charge you the greater of two rates: the cost based on weight or the cost based on a formula to determine the equivalent weight of a package based on its size: *(Length x Width x Height) ÷ 166* (for US domestic shipments; other factors apply for other countries and exports). Therefore, if you have a large package that doesn't weigh much, the live rate quoted in Magento might not be reflective of your actual cost once the dimensional weight is calculated. If your packages may be large and lightweight, consult your carrier representative or shipping fulfillment partner for guidance.

- If your shipping calculations need more sophistication than provided natively in Magento 2, consider an add-on. However, remember that what you charge your customers does *not* have to be what you pay. For that reason, and to keep it simple for your customers, consider offering **Table rates** (as described later in this chapter).
- Each method you choose will be displayed to your customers if their cart and shipping destination matches the conditions of the method. Take care not to confuse your customers with too many choices: simpler is better.

Keeping these insights in mind, let's explore the various shipping methods available by default in Magento 2.

Before we go over the shipping methods, let's go over some basic concepts that will apply to most, if not all, shipping methods.

Origin

From where you ship your products will determine the shipping rates, especially the carrier rates (for example, UPS and FedEx). To set your origin, go to **Stores | Configuration | Sales | Shipping Settings**, and expand the **Origin** panel. At the very least, enter the **Country**, **Region/State**, and **ZIP/Postal Code** field. The others are optional for rate calculation purposes.

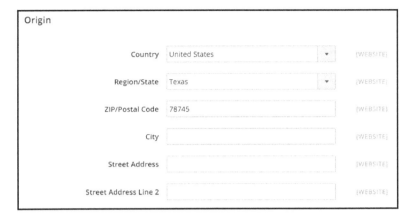

At the bottom of this panel is the choice to **Apply custom Shipping Policy**. If enabled, a field will appear where you can enter text about your overall **Shipping Policy**. For instance, you may want to enter `Orders placed by 12:00 pm CT will be processed for shipping on the same day. Applies only to orders placed Monday-Friday, excluding shipping holidays.`

Handling fee

You can add an *invisible handling fee* to all shipping rate calculations. Invisible in that it does not appear as a separate line item charge to your customers. To add a handling fee to a shipping method:

- Choose whether you wish to add a fixed amount or a percentage of the shipping cost.
- If you choose to add a percentage, enter the amount as a decimal number instead of a percentage (for example, 0.06 instead of 6%).

Allowed countries

As you configure your shipping methods, don't forget to designate the countries you will ship to. If you only ship to the US and Canada, for instance, be sure to have only those countries selected. Otherwise, you'll have customers from other countries placing orders that you will have to cancel and refund.

Method not available

In some cases, the method you configured may not be applicable to a customer based on destination, type of product, weight, or any number of factors. For these instances, you can choose to:

- Show the method (for example, UPS, USPS, DHL, and so on), but with an error message that the method is not applicable.
- Don't show the method at all.

Depending on your shipping destinations and target customers, you may want to show an error message just so the customer knows why no shipping solution is being displayed. If you don't show any error message and the customer does not qualify for any shipping method, the customer will be confused.

Free shipping

There are several ways to offer *free shipping* to your customers. If you want to display a **Free Shipping** option to all customers whose carts meet a minimum order amount (not including taxes or shipping), enable this panel.

However, you may want to be more judicious in how and when you offer free shipping. Other alternatives include the following:

- Creating shopping cart promotions (see `Chapter 8`, *Promotions and Communication*)
- Including a free shipping method in your **Table Rates** (see later in this section)
- Designating a specific free shipping method and minimum qualifying amount within a carrier configuration (such as UPS and FedEx)

If you choose to use this panel, note that it will apply to all orders. Therefore, if you want to be more selective, consider one of the preceding methods.

Flat rate

As with the **Free Shipping** panel, the **Flat Rate** panel allows you to charge one, singular flat rate for all orders regardless of weight or destination. You can apply the rate on a per-item or per-order basis as well.

Table rates

While using live carrier rates can provide more accurate shipping quotes for your customers, you may find it more convenient to offer a series of rates for your customers at certain break points.

For example, you might only need something as simple as the following for any domestic destination:

- 0-5 lbs, $5.99
- 6-10 lbs, $8.99
- 11+ lbs, $10.99

Let's assume you're a US-based shipper. While these rates will work for you when shipping to any of the contiguous 48 states, you need to charge more for shipments to Alaska and Hawaii. For our example, let's assume a tiered pricing of $7.99, $11.99, and $14.99 at the same weight breaks.

All of these conditions can be handled using the **Table Rates** shipping method. Based on our example, we would first start by creating a spreadsheet (in Excel or Numbers) similar to the following:

Country	Region/State	Zip/Postal Code	Weight (and above)	Shipping Price
USA	*	*	0	5.99
USA	*	*	6	8.99
USA	*	*	11	10.99
USA	AK	*	0	7.99
USA	AK	*	6	11.99
USA	AK	*	11	14.99
USA	HI	*	0	7.99
USA	HI	*	6	11.99
USA	HI	*	11	14.99

Let's review the columns in this chart:

- **Country**: Here, you would enter the three-character country code (for a list of valid codes, see `http://goo.gl/6A1woj`).
- **Region/State**: Enter the two-character code for any state or province.
- **Zip/Postal Code**: Enter the specific postal codes for which you wish the rate to apply.
- **Weight (and above)**: Enter the minimum applicable weight for the range. The assigned rate will apply until the weight of the cart products combined equals a higher weight tier.
- **Shipping Price**: Enter the shipping charge you wish to provide to the customer. Do not include the currency prefix (such as $ or €).

Now, let's discuss the asterisk (*), and how to limit the scope of your rates. As you can see in the chart, we have only indicated the rates for US destinations. That's because there are no rows for any other countries. We could easily add rates for *all other countries*, simply by adding rows with an asterisk in the first column. By adding those rows, we're telling Magento to use the US rates if the customer's ship-to address is in the US, and to use other rates for all other country destinations.

Likewise for the states column: Magento will first look for matches for any state codes listed. If it can't find any, then it will look for any rates with an asterisk. If no asterisk is present for a qualifying weight, then no applicable rate will be provided to the customer.

The asterisk in the Zip/Postal Code column means that the rates apply to all postal codes for all states.

 To get a sample file with which to configure your rates, you can set your configuration scope to one of your websites (Furniture or Sportswear in our examples), and click on **Export CSV** in the **Table Rates** panel.

Quantity and price-based rates

In the previous example, we used the weight of the items in the cart to determine the shipping rates. You can also configure table rates to use calculations based on the number of items in the cart or the total price of all items (less taxes and shipping).

To set up your chart, simply rename the fourth column Quantity (and above) or Subtotal (and above).

Save your rate table

To upload your table rates, you'll need to save/export your spreadsheet as a CSV file. You can name it whatever you like. Save it to your computer where you can find it for the next steps.

Table rate settings

Before you upload your new rates, you should first set your **Table Rates** configurations. To do so, you can set your default settings in the Default configuration scope. However, to upload your CSV file, you will need to switch your **Store View** to the appropriate Website scope.

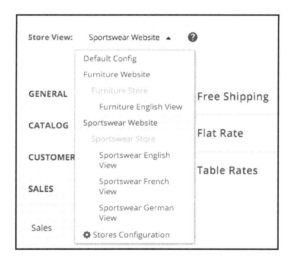

When changing to a Website scope, you will see the **Export CSV** button and the ability to upload your rate table file. You'll note that all other settings may have the **Use Default** box checked. You can, of course, uncheck this box beside any field, and adjust the settings according to your preferences.

Let's review the unique fields in this panel.

- **Enabled**: Set to **Yes** to enable **Table Rates**.
- **Title**: Enter the name you wish to be displayed to customers when they're presented with a table rate-based shipping charge in the checkout process.
- **Method Name**: This name is presented to the customer in the shopping cart.

You should probably change the default **Table Rate** to something more descriptive, as this term would likely be irrelevant to customers. We have used terms `Standard Ground`, `Economy`, or `Saver` as names. The **Title** should probably be the same as well so that the customer has a visual confirmation of their shipping choice during checkout.

- **Condition:** This allows you to choose the calculation method you want to use. Your choices, as we described earlier, are **Weight vs. Destination**, "**Price vs. Destination**, and # **of items vs. Destination**.
- **Include Virtual Products in Price Calculation**: Since virtual products (see `Chapter 5`, *Products*) have no weight, this will have no effect on the calculations for weight-based rates. However, it will affect calculations for price or quantity-based rates.

Once you have your settings, click on **Save Config**.

Upload rate table

Once you have saved your settings, you can now click on the button next to **Import,** and upload your rate table. Be sure to test your rates to see that you have properly constructed your rate table.

Carrier methods

The remaining shipping methods involve configuring UPS, USPS, FedEx, and/or DHL to provide *live* rate calculations. UPS is the only one that is set to query for live rates *without* the need for you to have an account with the carrier. This is both good and bad. It's good, as you only have to enable the shipping method to have it begin querying rates for your customers. On the flip side, the rates that are returned are not *negotiated rates*. Negotiated rates are those you may have been offered as discounted rates based on your shipping volume.

FedEx, USPS, and DHL require account-specific information in order to activate. This connection with your account should provide rates based on any discounts that you have established with your carrier. If you wish to use negotiated rates for UPS, you may have to find a Magento add-on that will accommodate or have your developer *extend* your Magento installation to make a modified rate query.

If you have some history with shipping, you should negotiate rates with the carriers. We have found most are willing to offer some discount from the published rates.

Shipping integrations

Unless you have your own sophisticated warehouse operation, it may be wise to partner with a fulfillment provider that can not only store, pick, pack, and ship your orders, but also offers deep discounts on shipping rates due to their large volumes.

Amazon FBA (Fulfillment By Amazon) is a very popular solution. Shipping is a low flat rate, based on weight (`http://goo.gl/UKjg7`).

ShipWire is another fulfillment provider that is well integrated with Magento. In fact, their integration can provide real-time rate quotes for your customers based on the products selected, warehouse availability, and destination (`http://www.ShipWire.com`). We have not heard if they have updated their integration for Magento 2 yet, but we suspect they will.

Customer groups

One of the little used, and understood, features of Magento is *customer groups*. Many online businesses need to provide special pricing or other considerations for groups of customers. Magento, by default, creates groups for the most common intentions such as the following:

- **General**: These are consumers who have registered with your site, either separately or as part of the checkout process.
- **NOT LOGGED IN**: As the name suggests, these are customers visiting your site who are not logged into their customer account (and who may not have an account established yet).
- **Retailer**: A customer who is buying products from you as a reseller. You are the wholesaler or distributor, and the customer is making the final sale to the end consumer.

- **Wholesale**: Someone who buys from you to resell to other vendors.

Using customer groups

Depending on your business intentions, you may require that all customers register with your site, and having done so (and been approved by you), are eligible to purchase at wholesale, non-taxed prices. You may be selling to both consumers and resellers. Another scenario might be that you want to offer different prices to consumers who are registered with your site, and those who are logged-in to view special pricing.

Carefully thinking about your customers may lead you to need additional groups other than the defaults. Perhaps you want different tiers or customers: Preferred and Non-Preferred, for instance. By creating multiple groups, you can assign customers, as they register, according to your classification criteria.

In Chapter 5, *Products*, we'll show how you can set pricing according to the customer group.

Aside from pricing and promotions, one key purpose for creating customer groups is for assigning customers based on taxing rules. If you sell globally, you may have customers who are in the **European Union** (**EU**), and for whom a VAT ID is required. Customers can be assigned to groups based on whether they are domestic, inter-union, and if they have a valid or invalid VAT ID.

We will discuss VAT tax later in this chapter, but if you're going to be charging VAT taxes, you should create four new customer groups:

- Domestic
- Intra-EU
- Invalid VAT ID
- Validation Error

These will be used to assign customers based on the validation of their VAT ID.

If you will not be selling from or to an EU member country, you should not have to be concerned with VAT taxes. However, as with any taxation question, you should consult qualified professionals.

Adding a customer group

To add a new customer group:

1. Go to **Stores | Customer Groups**.
2. Click on **Add New Customer Group**.
3. Enter the **Group Name,** and select the appropriate **Tax Class**.
4. Click on **Save Customer Group**.

You've no doubt noted that your Magento installation may only have one Tax Class. Of course, wholesale and resale customers should probably not be taxed on purchases (depending on local laws). Don't fret, we'll discuss taxes more in this chapter.

As we go through other configurations and processes in this book, you may discover new and creative ways to use customer groups.

Assigning VAT customer groups

Now that you have the default VAT-related customer groups created, you should configure new customer account settings to assign customers to these groups.

Go to **Stores** | **Configuration** | **Customers** | **Customer Configuration**, and expand the **Create New Accounts Options** panel.

1. Change **Enable Automatic Assignment to Customer Group** to **Yes**.
2. Select an option for **Tax Calculation Based On** depending on whether VAT should be calculated based on the billing or shipping address of the purchaser. If a customer buys a digital product, such as software, music or some other virtual product, VAT will be calculated on the billing address of the customer.
3. Select the **Default Group** for your customers (usually **General**).
4. Select **Domestic** for **Group for Valid VAT ID – Domestic**.
5. Select **Intra-EU** for **Group for Valid VAT ID – Intra-Union**.
6. Select **Invalid VAT ID** for **Group for Invalid VAT ID**.
7. Select **Validation Error** for **Validation Error Group**.
8. If you want Magento to automatically change group assignments based on any changes in the customer's VAT address, select **Yes** for **Default Value for Disable Automatic Group Changes Based on VAT ID**.
9. If you want to display your VAT ID on the front end of your store, you should select **Yes** for **Show VAT Number on Storefront**.

 Remember, if you're not responsible for VAT taxes, making these selections may have less-than-desired results in terms of customer group assignments.

Managing taxes

The great unavoidable: taxes. If you're a retailer, and even as a wholesaler in some jurisdictions, you will need to master the management of tax rates and rules in your Magento store. We've had to deal with this issue on many other platforms, and while some do provide some cool features, none, in our opinion, offer as much flexibility for taxes as Magento. Especially when it comes to VAT taxes.

 As you'll appreciate while going through this section, taxes can be quite complicated. Before configuring taxes in your online store, you should consult your tax professional. Making errors in taxes can not only present legal issues for your business, it can erode consumer confidence if customers feel they're being inappropriately taxed on purchases.

How Magento manages taxes

Taxes are applied to products based on assigned **Tax Classes**. Tax Classes are combined with **Tax Zones and Rates** to create **Tax Rules**. Tax Rules are what are applied to each product or shopping cart to determine the amount of tax charged in a transaction.

The following is a flow chart on how Magento calculates sales taxes based on a Tax Rule:

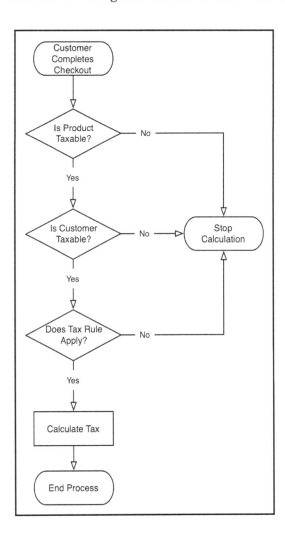

There are two types of Tax Classes in Magento:

- **Product Tax Class**: A product is usually considered taxable or non-taxable. If a product is not to be taxed, a value of "None" is selected for its tax class. You may find it necessary to have different product tax classes if you have different taxing rules for different products.
- **Customer Tax Class**: As we saw while creating Customer Groups, customers are assigned to a tax class, usually based on whether they are retail or wholesale customers.

Creating tax rules

Tax rules are created based on jurisdiction and rate: creating a zone for a country, state, and/or ZIP code, and a percentage used to calculate the tax.

To illustrate, let's review a tax rule included in the default installation for Magento 2.

1. Go to **Stores** | **Tax Rules** in your Magento backend.
2. Click on **Rule 1** listed in the Tax Rules table.

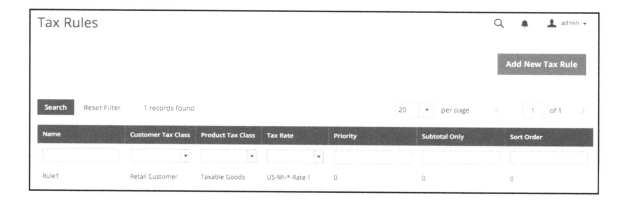

Name	Customer Tax Class	Product Tax Class	Tax Rate	Priority	Subtotal Only	Sort Order
Rule1	Retail Customer	Taxable Goods	US-MI-*-Rate 1	0	0	0

Let's now take a look at the layout of a Tax Rule:

- **Name**: While **Rule 1** is fine, it's not really descriptive, particularly in a list of rules. You can name the rule whatever you feel works best for you.
- **Tax Rate**: This field allows you to select one or more rates that you want to apply to the rule. You might have to apply several tax rates if you have multiple distribution locations or "nexuses." The rate is determined by the location of the buyer, usually their *Ship To* address.

> A nexus is generally considered if you have an active business in a particular state or locality. For instance, if your office is in Texas, and you ship your products from a warehouse in Illinois, then, for taxing purposes, you're considered to have a nexus in Texas and Illinois. Therefore, as it stands at this moment, you are required to collect sales tax on any sales to buyers in Texas and Illinois. However, there are efforts in the United States Congress to radically change taxing laws on online sales transactions. Some state legislatures are also grappling with this issue. We know you're used to hearing this, but you do need to consult a tax professional to make sure you're correctly charging sales tax.

You can add or edit Tax Rates here or under **Stores | Tax Zones and Rates**. Let's edit the California tax rate here to understand the process:

In the preceding screenshot, when you hover your mouse over the item **US-CA-*-Rate 1**, you will see a pencil icon to the right of the item name. Click on this to reveal the Tax Rate *modal dialogue*.

- **Tax Identifier**: You can enter whatever you wish in this space. The naming scheme shown was created by Magento in setting up this default rate.

- **Zip/Post is Range**: By checking this box, the **Zip/Post Code** field is replaced by range fields into which you can enter a starting and ending code range. This is particularly useful if you need to apply a different rate to a range of zip codes within a larger region.

Zip/Post is Range	✓
Range From ＊	
Range To ＊	

- **Zip/Post Code**: As indicated, an asterisk is considered a *wild card*. That is, any value will match. If you want to, for example, apply the rate to all zip codes beginning with 78 (that is, 78001, 78002, and so on), you could enter `78*`.
- **State**: Select the State for which the rate applies. The selections will change based on your country selection. An asterisk in this selection will apply the rate to all states and regions within the country.
- **Country**: Select the country for which the rate applies.
- **Rate Percent**: Enter the rate to be applied as a percentage amount. In other words, if the rate is 8.25%, enter `8.25`, not `0.0825`.
- **Tax Titles**: As in so many places in Magento, you can specifically name this item as you would like it to appear in your various store views. You might, for instance, wish to call the rule `CA Sales Tax` for your English views, but `CA La Taxe De Vente` for your French store view. If you leave any of these blank, your customer will be shown the Tax Identifier value.

You can use the same field specifics for creating a new tax rate by clicking on **Add New Tax Rate** at the bottom of the Tax Rate list field.

To view the remaining fields, expand the **Additional Settings** section.

- **Customer Tax Class**: As discussed earlier, **Customer Tax Classes** allow you to assign customer groups to different tax groups. For instance, you will probably have the sales taxes apply only to retail customers.

Wholesale Customer Tax Class

In Magento 2, there is no one place to go to create Customer Tax Classes. Therefore, you should create a "Wholesale Customer" tax class in any tax rule so that it will be available to you when managing Customer Groups.

- **Product Tax Class**: If you need additional **Product Tax Classes**, you can also add them here, and they will be available for selection in product edit panels.

- **Priority**: If you have more than one tax rate that might apply to a customer's shopping cart, those with the same priority will be *added*. That is, each tax rule will be calculated separately, then added together. If the priorities are different, then the rates will be *compounded* in order of priority. Let's take an example: you have two taxes that will apply to a product, a federal excise tax of 5% and a state sales tax of 8%. If the priorities for both are the same, the shopper's purchase of $100 will be taxed a total of $13-$5 for 5% and $8 for 8%. If you put a priority of 1 for the excise tax and a priority of 2, for instance, for the state sales tax, then the customer is taxed $13.40-$5 for the excise tax and $8.40 for the 8% of $105 ($100 plus the $5 excise tax). The latter is an example of **compounded sales tax**. Taxes with different priorities will also be listed as separate tax line items to your customers.

- **Calculated Off Subtotal Only**: Now, take what we just said about **Priority** and consider this: if you want each applicable tax, such as GST and PST taxes in Canada, to be displayed separately to the customer, each tax must have a different **Priority**. However, suppose you don't want these taxes compounded, as explained earlier. Therefore, to prevent compounding, yet have the tax shown as a separate line item, check this box. Now the tax will only be applied to the order subtotal, and not as a compounded tax calculation.

- **Sort Order**: If you have more than one applied tax, you can control the order in which they are listed to your customers. This will not change any compounding based on priority.

Importing tax rates

While you can't import Tax Rules, you can import **Tax Rates**, which may be a time saver, particularly where you have multiple taxing jurisdictions to whom you have to report the tax collections.

As with many importing capabilities in Magento 2, the easiest way to begin is by exporting the current tax rules and expanding on the CSV file, then importing your changes. To import tax rates, view any Tax Rule. At the bottom of the screen are buttons to import and export tax rates. Export the current tax rate file, add or edit your rates, then reimport.

Value added tax configurations

In some countries, goods and services are taxed in a means similar to sales tax, but calculated and managed differently. These **Value Added Taxes** (**VAT**) are made even more complex due to the varying rates among countries, different rules for registration, and rules for taxation based on the type of product or service sold.

 As usual, we can't begin to counsel you on taxes. VAT rules can be complicated, especially for non-EU countries selling into EU countries. We strongly suggest you consult your tax professionals. If you doubt the complexity of EU VAT taxes, see http://goo.gl/y07Pb.

The VAT process in Magento involves three basic components, the need for any of these is based on your location:

- **VAT Validation**: For customers who provide a VAT ID, Magento 2 is able to query the European Commission to verify their VAT ID
- **VAT Tax Rules**: As with sales taxes, the creation of tax rules based on certain conditions or considerations
- **System Configuration**: Activate the rules that will manage VAT-eligible purchases

In Magento, VAT is charged if both the seller and customer are located in the same EU country. If both are EU-registered businesses, no VAT tax is collected if the seller and customer are in different countries.

When selling to consumers in EU countries, the amount of VAT collected is based on what country the seller is located in (if the seller is a EU country). These are called **Intra-EU sales**.

One exception (there's always one, yes?) is that when selling digital goods (like music, software, and so on), the VAT rate to be charged is that of the destination country, not the source country.

The key to effectively manage this complexity is the creation of multiple customer groups that can be automatically assigned during the checkout or registration process based on the VAT ID validation of the buyer.

Setup VAT taxes

It would be so easy for us to stop here, call it a day, and leave VAT tax configuration to your imagination. After all, we can play the "too complex for a book" card, correct?

The truth is that VAT taxes can be quite complex. If you're an EU business or exporting to the EU countries, you already understand the complexities. However, we do want you to get the most from Magento 2, and demonstrate its incredible ability to fulfill your tax calculation needs.

To that end, and perhaps the best way to demonstrate the process, we're going to set up VAT taxes as if we were a business based in France (we love Paris!).

Since we're considered, in this example, as an EU member country, we will need to provide for VAT ID validation of our customers, and classify them accordingly.

Earlier in this chapter, we added four additional Customer Groups, specifically for VAT tax use. If we look under **Stores** | **Customer Groups**, based on our example Magento install, we should see the following:

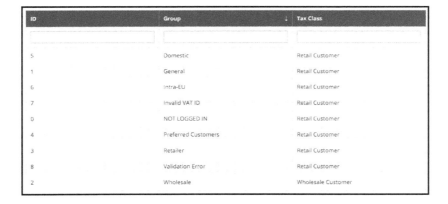

ID	Group	Tax Class
5	Domestic	Retail Customer
1	General	Retail Customer
6	Intra-EU	Retail Customer
7	Invalid VAT ID	Retail Customer
0	NOT LOGGED IN	Retail Customer
4	Preferred Customers	Retail Customer
3	Retailer	Retail Customer
8	Validation Error	Retail Customer
2	Wholesale	Wholesale Customer

Next, we have to create the product classes that we will need for applying the appropriate French VAT tax rates. France groups products into four rate categories, each of which should have a different product class added for taxing purposes:

 All tax rates and information shown here are for illustrative purposes only, and *should not be used without validation*.

- **Standard VAT**: These will be taxed at 20%.
- **Reduced VAT 1**: Applies to books, transportation, entertainment events, and hotels. Taxed at 10%.
- **Reduced VAT 2**: Applies to medical, food, and book products. Taxed at 5.5%.
- **Reduced VAT 3**: Applies to newspaper and pharmaceuticals. Taxed at 2.1%.

We now have to consider that for customers living in other EU countries, we will charge our VAT tax rate on purchases of physical products, but charge the buyers, VAT tax rate for digital or virtual purchases.

That means that if we are selling digital products (like, music, software, and so on) to other EU customers, we have to charge VAT tax at the rate in their country, not France. In order to do that, we have to add Tax Rates in Magento for every other EU country. As you can imagine, setting up all those tax rates and rules can be quite time consuming.

We have created a CSV file of all EU countries with their standard VAT tax rates (as of this writing). You can use this to upload the tax rates to your Magento 2 install.

For France, we need to create the four tax rates described previously. After adding these under **Stores | Tax Zones and Rates** in our Magento 2 backend, the list of tax rates looks like the following image:

France Reduced VAT 1	France	*	*	10.00
France Reduced VAT 2	France	*	*	5.5
France Reduced VAT 3	France	*	*	2.1
France Standard	France	*	*	20.00

Our next chore is to create the Product Tax classes that are needed to segregate our products according to the taxes we have to apply. For our France-based example, we will need five Product Tax Classes:

- **Standard**: These are physical products and services that don't fall into the other product classes
- **Reduced Tax Class 1**: In France, these include passenger transportation, events (sports and entertainment), hotels, and restaurants
- **Reduced Tax Class 2**: Medical, food, and books
- **Reduced Tax Class 3**: Newspapers and pharmaceuticals
- **Virtual Products**: Music, software, and other "non-physical" products

While you may not currently sell products that fall into all of these classes, you may want to go ahead, and set them up so they're available to you.

Remember, to create additional Product Tax Classes, just click to edit any Tax Rule, expand **Additional Settings**, and add your new classes. After adding the previously mentioned classes, this section will look like the following screenshot:

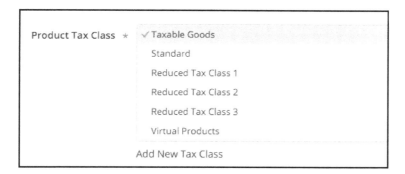

With the preceding preparation completed, we can now create the Tax Rules that will be used to calculate VAT taxes on purchases. We need to create the following Tax Rules to meet our needs as a French online business:

1. Domestic customers purchasing **Standard** products.
2. Domestic customers purchasing **Reduced Tax Class 1** products.
3. Domestic customers purchasing **Reduced Tax Class 2** products.
4. Domestic customers purchasing **Reduced Tax Class 3** products.
5. All customers purchasing **Virtual** products.
6. Intra-EU customers purchasing **non-Virtual** products.

Once entered into our Magento 2 example, our Tax Rules screen would include the following:

Domestic Customer - Standard	Retail Customer	Standard	France Standard	0	0	0
Domestic Customer - Reduced 1	Retail Customer	Reduced Tax Class 1	France Reduced VAT 1	0	0	0
Domestic Customer - Reduced 2	Retail Customer	Reduced Tax Class 2	France Reduced VAT 2	0	0	0
Domestic Customer - Reduced 3	Retail Customer	Reduced Tax Class 3	France Reduced VAT 3	0	0	0
EU Customer - Virtual	Retail Customer	Virtual Products	Austria, Belgium, Bulgaria, Coratia, Cyprus, Czech Republic, Denmark, Estonia, Finland, France Standard, Germany, Greece, Hungary, Ireland, Italy, Latvia, Lithuania, Luxembourg, Malta, Netherlands, Poland, Portugal, Romania, Slovakia, Slovenia, Spain, Sweden, United Kingdom	0	0	0
Intra-EU Customer - Non-Virtual	Retail Customer	Standard, Reduced Tax Class 1, Reduced Tax Class 2, Reduced Tax Class 3	Austria, Belgium, Bulgaria, Coratia, Cyprus, Czech Republic, Denmark, Estonia, Finland, Germany, Greece, Hungary, Ireland, Italy, Latvia, Lithuania, Luxembourg, Malta, Netherlands, Poland, Portugal, Romania, Slovakia, Slovenia, Spain, Sweden, United Kingdom	0	0	0

Remember, we are *not* tax experts. Your tax rules may differ from the example shown. The purpose of this exercise is to demonstrate the various steps needed to add VAT tax calculations to a Magento 2 store.

The final piece is to configure your Customer Configuration so that customers are automatically assigned to the proper Customer Group based on their VAT ID validation. To do that, go to **Stores** | **Configuration** | **Customers** | **Customer Configuration**, and expand the **Create New Account Options** panel. Some of these settings are done at the Global, Website, and Store View levels, so pay close attention to your **Store View** scope setting in the upper-right part of the screen. For our example, we only want to automatically assign customers who visit our French store. Therefore, we will only enable this feature at the **Sportswear French View**.

Once you have changed to the appropriate Store View level, the key fields to configure are the following:

- **Enable Automatic Assignment to Customer Group**: Set to **Yes**, and Magento will reveal additional configuration fields.
- **Tax Calculation Based On**: Usually, you will set this to **Shipping Address** so that taxes are based on the customer's taxing jurisdiction, although there are exceptions.
- **Default Group**: At the Store View level, you may want to set this to **Domestic**.
- **Group for Valid VAT ID – Domestic**: Set to your domestic group, **Domestic**.
- **Group for Valid VAT ID – Intra-Union**: Set to **Intra-EU**.
- **Group of Invalid VAT ID**: Set to **Invalid VAT ID**.
- **Validation Error Group**: Set to **Validation Error** as the Customer Group.
- **Validate on Each Transaction**: If you're going to calculate VAT taxes, then you would most like set this to **Yes**.
- **Default Value for Disable Automatic Group Changes Based on VAT ID**: This feature allows Magento to reassign customers if their VAT ID or address changes. If you do not want this feature, set this to **Yes**.

As with any store configuration, especially one as complex as VAT taxes, we highly recommend that you test your configurations thoroughly.

Managing orders

Now that you're configured to allow customers to complete their purchases, let's turn our attention to what happens *after* the sale: the order process.

Magento 2 has a carefully crafted process for how orders flow from checkout to shipment. Once we understand the "core" flow, we can begin to explore how changes to orders, such as cancellations and refunds, fall into this process.

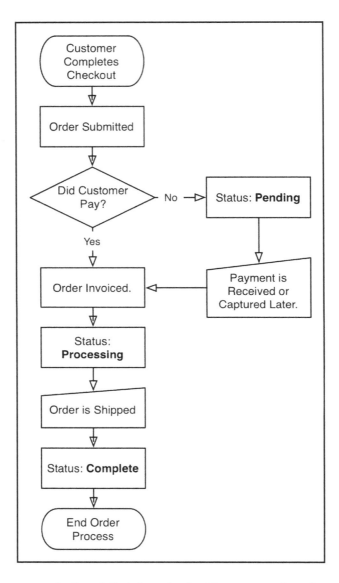

To understand this process better, let's take a look at two examples of new orders in the Magento 2 backend. Orders are accessed by going to **Sales** | **Orders** in the Magento backend.

	ID ↑	Purchase Point	Purchase Date	Bill-to Name	Ship-to Name	Grand Total (Base)	Grand Total (Purchased)	Status	Action
☐	000000003	Sportswear Website Sportswear Store Sportswear English View	Dec 6, 2015 10:46:11 PM	Veronica Costello	Veronica Costello	$53.71	$53.71	Pending	View
☐	000000002	Sportswear Website Sportswear Store Sportswear English View	Nov 21, 2015 11:53:18 PM	Veronica Costello	Veronica Costello	$37.00	$37.00	Complete	View
☐	000000001	Sportswear Website Sportswear Store Sportswear English View	Nov 21, 2015 11:53:17 PM	Veronica Costello	Veronica Costello	$34.00	$34.00	Processing	View

The first order shown, **000000003**, is an order paid for by check or money order. Since the funds have not yet been received, it has a status of **Pending**. The second order in the list, **000000002**, was also paid by check, but the money was received. The order is shown as **Complete,** because the order has been shipped. Finally, the last order in the list is shown as **Processing** because the payment has been received, but the order has not yet been marked Complete (in the Sample Data, this order has been shipped, though).

Before shipping an order to a customer, you will usually want to be paid. There may be times, such as wholesale customers paying via Purchase Order, that you may decide to ship before receiving payment, but in most cases, receiving a payment is required before shipping products to a customer.

Processing a shipment

Let's work first on order**000000003**. If we click on **View**, we see the details of the order. At the top of the order panel, we see a variety of actions we can take on this order. These actions will appear when an action is *eligible*. For instance, if you have already invoiced an order, **Invoice** will not appear in this top menu.

Let's discuss what each of these actions do.

By clicking on **Back**, you will be returned to your previous screen.

Cancel will cancel the order. You cannot cancel an order for which a payment has been received. In order to do that, you must first issue a **Credit Memo** (which appears in this menu in these cases). We'll discuss credit memos a bit later in this chapter.

Send Email will send a copy of the order (or invoice, shipment, or credit memo, depending on the panel you're at) to the customer.

Hold will change the status of the order to *Hold*, which means that it will not be processed for payment or shipment. In some cases, you may need to hold an order, particularly if you suspect fraud.

When you receive payment for an order, you can click on **Invoice**. Depending on your configuration, online payments by credit card or payment service (like PayPal) may automatically invoice an order. Once invoiced, this menu will not appear.

Capture Payment appears when the customer pays using a payment gateway, and you have configured the gateway to only *authorize* the payment instead of *authorize and capture*. This sends a message to the payment gateway to proceed with charging the customer's credit card or payment method, and converts the order to a paid invoice.

If you're handling shipping of products on your own, and you're not using a third-party shipping tool, such as ShipStation (`www.shipstation.com`), you can record the shipment by clicking on **Ship**.

As a service to your customers, they can also look up a past order, and click on **Reorder** to generate a new order that includes the same products as the older order. The customer will still be able to modify the new order, but this can be a real time-saver.

And, finally, you can **Edit** an order that is still in Pending status. But, before you make that choice, let's discuss its implications.

Editing an order

Without clicking **Edit** in the top menu of a pending order, you can still edit the customer's billing and shipping addresses. This can be useful if a customer realizes upon receipt of their order confirmation e-mail that they made a mistake.

However, clicking on **Edit** does not mean you can edit any other aspects of the order. In fact, by clicking on **Edit**, the customer is given a modal dialogue that notifies them that the current order will be cancelled, and a new order created.

We've had so many people ask us why Magento requires cancellation of the current order, and the creation of a new order. It has to do with data integrity and workflow. Rather than create what would undoubtedly be a very complex mechanism for editing an existing order of products, prices, and so on, and since a pending order has not been invoiced or shipped, it's easier for Magento to cancel the current order, and create a new order based on the information of the existing order.

Invoicing an order

When you have a pending order for which payment is received, you can record that payment by clicking on Invoice in the top menu. Let's use Order **000000003** as an example.

On the order detail screen, click on **Invoice** in the top menu. You will be taken to the Invoice screen. Here, you can enter the number of items that are being paid for in each line item of the order. By default, the quantity ordered is already entered.

The **Invoice History** will show any payments that have been received via payment gateways. For checks or money orders received, you should enter the payment details in the **Invoice Comments** field for record-keeping purposes.

Once you're satisfied with the information, click on **Submit Invoice** to finalize the payment. You can check the boxes to send your comments or simply an invoice receipt via e-mail to your customer.

 Note that the Invoice # may not always match the Order #, and likewise for Shipment # and Credit Memo #. That's because you may have a single order with multiple payments, shipments, and/or credit memos. There are add-ons that will synchronize these numbers, though, by appending suffixes to multiple records.

Issuing a credit memo

When you need to refund all or a portion of an order to a customer, you can issue a **Credit Memo**. If the payment method is offline (such as check or money order), the refund is simply recorded manually. If the customer used an online payment method, and you wish to refund the amount back to their credit card or online account, you can do that as well. Magento takes care of sending the refund request back to the payment gateway, and recording the result of the transaction in the order.

Shipping an order

For many online retailers, shipping is handled through an outside party, such as a fulfillment center, drop shipper, or shipping software (like ShipStation). Some shippers, via integration with Magento, can automatically retrieve orders that are in the processing status, ship your products, and update Magento with tracking information. This action will also change the status of the order to **Complete**.

However, in those cases where you are doing your own shipping, you can also update your orders in the Magento backend. Let's go through that process, again using order **000000003**. At this point, the order has been invoiced, and its status changed to **Processing**.

 When you manually invoice a pending order, you can also check the box labeled **Create Shipment** to immediately process the shipment. Usually, however, you will invoice an order, and someone else in your shipping department will process shipments.

While your shipping process may vary somewhat, here's a typical shipping process:

1. If you wish to print out packing slips to give to your shipping crew, go to **Sales | Orders**. Select the orders you wish to ship, and in the drop-down menu at the top, select **Print Packing Slips**.

2. Once you have shipped your order, go into the details of the order (click **View** on the listed order).
3. Click on **Ship** in the top menu.
4. Click on **Add Tracking Number** in the **Shipping Information** area.

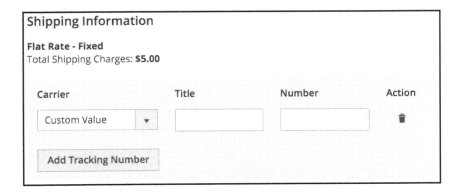

4. Choose the carrier used for the shipment, enter a **Title** (if you wish) of the service (for example, Ground), and the tracking number.

5. Confirm the number of each item that was shipped (*partial shipments* are allowed in Magento).

6. Select whether to send an e-mail update to your customer (and any comments you may wish to add).

7. Click on **Submit Shipment**.

Once you ship all the items in the order, the status of the order will change to **Complete**.

Practice makes perfect

Each business may have its own rules about how to process, ship, and refund orders. You should try as many different scenarios as you can before you activate your new Magento 2 store. Only then will you realize what you can and cannot do in Magento, or how you may want to add defined procedures to your order process.

If you find that you need some workflow that Magento 2 cannot accommodate by default, talk to your developer about possible add-ons that can add more functionality.

Summary

Selling is the primary purpose of building an online store. As you've seen in this chapter, Magento 2 arms you with a very rich array of features to help you give your customers the ability to purchase using a variety of payment methods. You're able to customize your shipping options, and manage complex tax rules. All of this combines to make it easy for your customers to complete their online purchases.

In Chapter 5, *Products*, we turn our attention to what your customers buy: understanding product types, managing inventory, pricing tools, increasing cart totals, and Special product management features.

As with any other aspect of Magento 2, creating products is both complex and, once mastered, rewarding.

5
Products

E-commerce is all about selling something. Whether it's t-shirts or car parts, consulting services or software, you're in the business of e-commerce to sell. If you look at the products you wish to sell, you may realize that you have several different types of products, too. Some may be simple, single products, such as a book, while others may be more complex, such as a shoe that comes in different sizes and colors.

Magento 2 gives you the power and capability to sell just about any type of product due to the incredible tools that it provides. We really haven't found another platform that is nearly as robust when it comes to supporting many different types of products so well.

In this chapter, we will:

- Learn about the different product types supported by Magento
- Dive into creating new products and attributes
- Discuss inventory management and configurations to meet your needs
- Explore pricing tools
- Discover additional product selling opportunities using cross-sells, upsells, and related products

As you go through this chapter, we know you'll think of new and innovative ways of presenting your products and services. That's part of the magic of Magento 2: it gives you the tools and platform for doing almost magical things to increase your online success.

Product types

If you think about products—the various products you do or want to sell online—you may quickly realize that your items are more complex than they seem at first glance. In fact, most products you can buy online require more than simply a photo, description, and price.

Let's explore the idea of **product types** for a moment, as it not only shapes the contents of this chapter, but may also give you some creative ideas.

Simple products

If you shop online for a ballpoint pen with blue ink, you could well find a list of pens where each ink color is a separate product. The individual pen products would be considered **Simple products**.

In Magento, we think of a Simple product as one for which there is a single **Stock Keeping Unit** (**SKU**). If the blueink pen has an SKU of PEN1234BLU, then we would build it in Magento as a Simple Product.

Simple Products can have **custom options**, though. For instance, we could offer this blueink pen in different ballpoint sizes, but with a Simple Product, we cannot assign different SKUs to each option. Therefore, if we are stocking each blueink pen in different ballpoint sizes, then we would need to create Simple Products for each variant.

 Variant is a common term used in e-commerce to describe related variations of a product. For example, a t-shirt that comes in S, M, and L sizes would be referred to as having three variants; each size would be a variant of the t-shirt.

The preceding screenshot illustrates a Simple Product. It has no other sizes or colors, and is not a bundle or group of products.

Simple products in Magento become the basis for all other tangible Complex product types, which we'll discuss in the next section. The important concept to learn here is that all tangible products begin with the Simple product type.

Complex products

When two or more simple products are combined in a single product representation, we are creating a **Complex product type**. In Magento, we also consider Virtual and Downloadable products as *complex* because of the additional considerations needed to manage non-tangible products.

The Configurable product type

Perhaps the most popular Complex product type is the **Configurable product type**. This type is used when you sell an item that comes in different sizes, colors, and so on. The most common example is clothing.

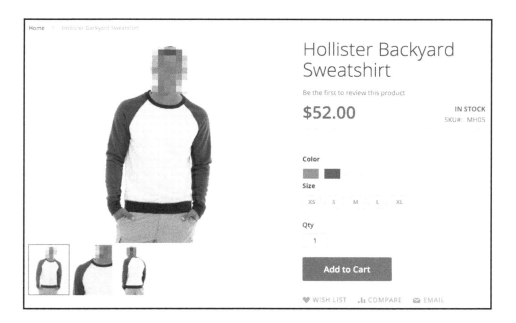

For example, the sweatshirt shown in the preceding screenshot, comes in three different colors and five different sizes. In Magento, there are actually two ways you can build out this product:

- You can build a simple product, and create options for the colors and sizes
- You can build simple products for each combination of color and size (for example, Red-Small, Red-Medium, White-Small, and so on), and present all the variations as a single Configurable product

The key to decide on the method to use boils down to how you answer the following questions:

1. Do you need to track inventory for each variant?
2. For all the colors and sizes of this item, will any of the possible combinations not be available (for example, you might not be able to source White-XL sweatshirts)?

If you answer yes to either of these questions, then you should use a Configurable product. You cannot track inventory on Custom Options (which we'll go into more detail later in this chapter), and for whatever Custom Options you create, customers will be able to choose all possible combinations.

Configurable products also give you tremendous content versatility. For example, with the sweatshirt product (included in the Magento 2 Sample Data), as the customer selects a different color, the main image changes to that of the associated Simple product image.

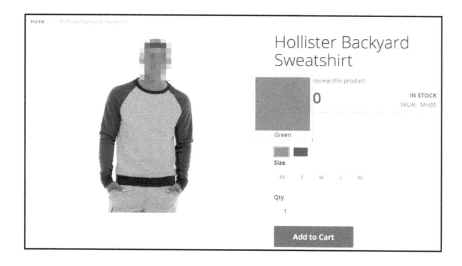

Furthermore, the stock available for each selected combination is shown to the customer. Any associated Simple Product that is not available will be indicated, as shown in the following screenshot (when **Red** is selected, the **XL** size is not available):

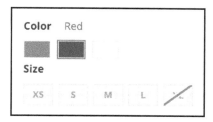

As we'll see when we create a Configurable Product type later, Magento 2 introduces new tools for rapidly creating the needed variants.

Grouped product type

Sometimes, it's helpful to display several different products as a related group to make it easier for customers to choose one or more products. The **Grouped product type** associates Simple or Virtual product types into one Complex product.

As shown in the preceding screenshot of sample Yoga Straps, the customer can choose any quantity of any of the products, which exist as Simple Products in your catalog. Each product chosen will appear separately in the customer's shopping cart.

 Keep in mind that a Grouped product cannot use Simple products that have Custom Options.

Bundle product type

A Complex product similar to the Grouped Product is the **Bundle product type**. Similar in that it associates Simple or Virtual products that do not have Custom Options, but different in that you can create a *base collection* of products for the bundle, and set a price for the combined items. You can also create additional options for the user to choose from, and allow the pricing to be determined *dynamically*. In the latter, the product listing will show a range of pricing based on the least expensive and most expensive possible configurations. There's a lot of versatility to the Bundle product type.

Although not completely supported, the Bundle product can be used to create what is often called a **kit**. When we use this term, it refers to the assembling of various individual products into a single presented product, usually priced at a discount from the sum of the individual product prices. Let's explore a possible scenario to better understand the concept of a kit.

We have a client who sells dictation related products. He wants to combine a digital recorder that retails for $500 with a transcription kit that retails for $400, and offer this combined kit for a special discounted price of $800, saving the customer $100. In addition, our client needs to maintain inventory counts for both items, so that if one goes out of stock, the bundle is, therefore, not in stock.

Using a Bundle product, our client can build this kit—or bundle—assigning it a special price, and yet maintain each one separately for inventory and shipping purposes.

 The big issue with using the bundle product type for kits is that, by default, the customer must still click to customize the bundle before adding it to their cart. Even though you may not have any options available for the customer, this extra step is still required. Look for innovative developers to create modifications that will alter this behavior.

Virtual product type

Just as the name implies, a **Virtual product type** is an intangible product. Typical Virtual products include subscriptions, memberships, and warranties.

Unlike tangible products, Virtual products have no shipping weight, and no shipping options will appear during the checkout process.

Downloadable product type

We live in a world of digital distribution. Books, music, and software are more commonly downloaded today than sent on CDs or—anyone remember these?—floppy disks.

In Magento, you can sell and distribute digital products using the **Downloadable product type**. When customers purchase the product, they are e-mailed links to files on your server or on another server. Customers can also access their Downloadable products when they log into their account on your store.

With a Downloadable product, you can set the maximum number of downloads you will allow a customer, and whether the link is shareable with others.

Product attributes

Before diving into the creation of products, we need to explore a very important and powerful feature of Magento: **product attributes**. We have yet to find another common platform that provides the level of sophistication for product attributes as well as Magento.

In Magento, every field related to a product is called an attribute. The description, price, weight, and SKU of a product are attributes. In fact, all the fields that appear by default on a product detail screen are attributes.

But the real power comes in those attributes that you can add to your product screens to capture more granular aspects of your products, such as color, size, kHz, and screen size. Obviously, not all attributes are relevant to all products. For instance, t-shirt size would not be applicable to your furniture products. Fabric would not be a useful attribute for computer monitors. And that's where Magento really shines!

If you view the **More Information** tab under the Sample Data product *Montana Wind Jacket*, for example, you will see four attributes listed, as shown in the following screenshot:

Each of these relevant attributes helps your customers get a better understanding of your products. You can certainly include this information in your product description field, but when you create attributes, your customers can use them for comparison purposes. It also makes it easier for you to make sure you have included all product specifications when creating new products in your store.

Furthermore, attributes can be used to create the **layered navigation** that appears in the sidebar on your category pages (if **Is Anchor** is set to **Yes**; see Chapter 4, *Preparing to Sell*), as shown in the following screenshot:

Only certain attribute types can be used in layered navigation: Multiple Select, Dropdown, Price, Visual Swatch, and Text Swatch. See the next section for more information on attribute types.

In your Magento 2 backend, go to **Stores** | **Product** (under the **Attributes** group heading).

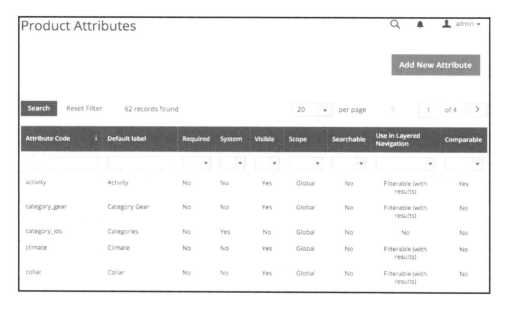

Here, you will see a listing of all the product attributes, both default and user added, that are available for your products.

To use attributes for creating products, you create **Attribute Sets** (also referred to as **Product Templates** in Magento 2) to group attributes into meaningful sets relevant to the various products you are offering. We'll explore Attribute Sets in a moment, once we learn how to create individual attributes.

Attribute types

Before we begin building or editing product attributes, let's learn about the different **attribute types** accommodated in Magento 2. Each has its own considerations and features.

Attributes are considered name-value pairs, meaning that for each attribute, there is a name, such as Size, and one or more values, such as Small, Medium, Large. The values you need for each attribute—and how you wish to use the attribute—is what helps you determine the type of attribute to create.

- **Text Field**: As the name implies, this attribute allows you to enter any text information you wish to describe the feature.
- **Text Area**: Similar to a text field, the text area field allows for a larger entry. Plus, you can use the WYSIWYG editor to style the content, insert HTML tags, or use other editing features.
- **Date**: You might have a product with a release date (such as a music album) or other date specific feature. Use the **Date** field to allow you to easily input a date using a pop-up calendar.
- **Yes/No**: As the name implies, it allows you to simply choose between **Yes** and **No** as values. This might be useful for *question* type features, such as Includes Power Cord? or Eligible for Extended Warranty?
- **Multiple Select**: This field type presents you a list of choices for the attribute. You can choose one or more from the list. You have full control over the items in the value list (as we'll see a bit later in this section).
- **Dropdown**: Similar to **Multiple Select**, except that you can only choose one from a list of possible choices.
- **Price**: You can create additional price fields for your products other than the **Price**, **Special Price**, **Tier Prices,** and **Cost** fields already present in Magento. While additional price fields aren't used during the checkout process, you could create fields to present prices for other reasons, such as Compare At or Sold in Stores At.
- **Media Image**: You can add additional image fields to your products in addition to the Base, Small, and Thumbnail images. You can exclude this new image from the thumbnail gallery, or allow it to be included.
- **Fixed Product Tax**: If you have a product that has a fixed tax amount, you could use this attribute type. The values entered would be included in any tax reporting or display based on your General Tax Settings (see Chapter 4, *Preparing to Sell*).

- **Visual Swatch**: A new feature in Magento 2, this field allows you to present the attribute as a color or image, such as a texture or cloth, as seen in the following screenshot:

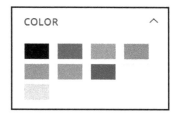

- **Text Swatch**: This new Magento 2 attribute type displays text as a button. You could use this for such things as shoe sizes or kHz.

Selecting an attribute type

Before you begin creating attributes, it's important to understand the implication of using one attribute type over another. Each type has its own particular abilities.

The one ability that is usually most important is whether or not the attribute can be used in layered navigation (as described earlier). For an attribute to be used as a layered attribute, it has to have fixed values. Magento indexes attributes, and it makes sense that it cannot provide layered navigation on free-form fields. Therefore, if you wish to use an attribute in layered navigation, it must be a **Multiple Select**, **Dropdown**, **Price**, **Visual Swatch**, or **Text Swatch** attribute type. Eligible attribute types can also be designated for use in the layered navigation of search results.

Another ability commonly considered for attributes is whether the attribute will be used when customers *compare products*. In the comparison display, only those attributes chosen for comparison will be shown side by side. All attribute types, except for **Media Image** and **Fixed Product Tax**, are eligible for use in comparisons.

Creating an attribute

We're going to create a new attribute to use for our furniture products called fabric, which will help us learn how to add new attributes. We want to use this value in layered navigation and for comparison purposes.

To begin, click on **Add New Attribute** at the top of the attribute list.

As with many configurations in Magento, the availability of certain fields and choices is often determined by other field choices. If some fields we discuss are not visible, it may be due to a previous choice.

Attribute properties

In the first panel, you'll find the following fields:

- **Default label**: Regardless of what you wish to have the attribute labeled on your store (which we'll discuss a bit later), you can name it for your backend use. In our example, we would enter `Fabric`.
- **Catalog Input Type for Store Owner**: Use this to select the type of attribute you wish to create (see previous section for more on attribute types).
- **Values Required**: If you wish to require that a value be entered or selected, choose **Yes**.
- **Update Product Preview Image**: For applicable Attribute Types, this will allow the main product image on a catalog listing page to display the related swatch value (applies only to the backend catalog listing).
- **Use Product Image for Swatch if Possible**: When using swatches in Configurable products, the product will display the swatches as selectors. When a swatch is selected, the main image can be replaced with the base image of the associated product.

Managing options

This section will only appear if you select **Multiple Select** or **Dropdown** as your Attribute Type (Catalog Input Type for Store Owner). For these attribute types, you have to provide the possible value choices. Let's take t-shirt size as an example. If you use a **Dropdown** type, you can enter all possible size choices—and make sure they're presented and spelled as you would like them to appear.

To create an option, click on **Add Option**. Enter the value you want for the option in the **Admin** column. If you want different displayed values for your multiple stores, enter those into the other fields. Any store views without a value will use the Admin column value.

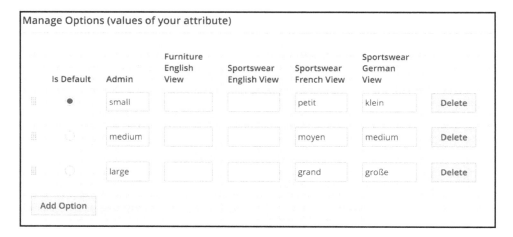

Once you have more than one value, you can choose which will be the default value when creating a new product by clicking on the **Is Default** radio button. You can also re-arrange the order of the values by clicking and dragging the handle on the left end of an option row.

Managing swatches

This section will be available if you choose a Visual or Text Swatch Attribute Type. Adding swatch options works very similarly to the options described earlier, except that you are working with swatches instead of option values.

Visual Swatches are configured by selecting either a color value or uploading an image of the swatch. Using the down arrow menu, select **Choose a Color** to reveal a color selector popup. You can move your mouse across the color spectrums, enter RGB or HSB numerical values, or enter a hexadecimal value to choose your color. Once you make your selection, click on the small, round rainbow-colored button in the lower right-hand corner of the selector.

If you choose **Upload a File** for your swatch, you can select a swatch image on your computer to upload.

If you use swatch images, try to create your swatches so that they're big enough to display enough texture, if that's important. For layout quality, your swatches should all be the same size.

Text swatches will display the values you enter as a button. The swatches will show all available values, and if any are out of stock or not available, it will appear crossed out.

Advanced attribute properties

Expand the **Attribute Properties** panel to reveal the following field choices:

- **Attribute Code**: This is an *internal* code used by Magento (and, perhaps, your developer if they customize your installation). Similar to a URL path, the key should be all lowercase, and not include spaces. If you don't enter one, Magento will create one automatically.

- **Scope**: Use this to decide whether the entry should apply to all products at the Global, Website, or Store level. For instance, if you select Global, then whatever is entered in your attribute for a product will apply at all scope levels, and cannot be changed at the Website or Store level.

- **Default Value**: If you want to have a default value displayed when the field is presented in a product edit screen, enter it here.

- **Unique Value**: There may be certain times you want a value to only apply to one product.

- **Input Validation for Store Owner**: You can have Magento validate whether a value entered meets certain requirements: decimal numbers (such as 12.43: a number with a decimal point), integer value (for example, 2 or 77: no decimal point), e-mail address, a URL (web address containing http or https), letters (a through z), or letters and number (a-z and 0-9). If the entry does not match the validation selection, the user will receive an error message.
- **Add to Column Options**: You can elect to have an attribute appear in the list of products when viewing the Catalog.
- **Use in Filter Options**: In addition, you can allow the backend user to filter listed products using your new attribute.

Managing labels

By default, your attribute will be named by the value you enter in the **Default label** field. However, if you want to display the name of your attribute on your store frontend, you may want to supply alternatives for each of your store views. For instance, if you create an attribute called screen size, you will probably want to translate it for the stores you build in other languages.

Storefront properties

This is the section that allows you to affect how your attribute can be used by your customers.

As noted earlier, different Attribute Types will determine what properties may or may not be available.

- **Use in Search**: When customers search for products on your site, you can include the values of this attribute as a search value. For example, you may have customers that often search for halogen light bulbs. If all your products have halogen in their title, no problem, but what if many of your products do not include halogen in the title? You could create an attribute called Bulb Type with halogen as one of the values. By setting this attribute field to **Yes,** if someone searches for halogen light bulbs, products with this attribute set to halogen would be included in the search results.

- **Comparable on Storefront**: You can select attributes to be included in the side-by-side product comparisons for your customers.

- **Use in Layered Navigation**: For applicable Attribute Types, you can choose to use them in the frontend layered navigation.

- **Use in Search Results Layered Navigation**: Likewise for layered navigation in search results.

- **Position**: If you do use an attribute in layered navigation, you can command its position relative to other attributes by entering a number in this field. Attributes will be shown in an ascending order (lowest to highest) according to this field.

- **Use for Promo Rule Conditions**: As we'll discuss later in Chapter 8, you can construct discounts and promotions based on the values of attributes for which this field is set to **Yes**.

- **Allow HTML Tags on Storefront**: For applicable Attribute Types, you can allow the use of HTML tags in the field value. For instance, you might want to make part of a value bold, such as `Contains <strong>EPA-Approved</strong> cleaners`.

- **Visible on Catalog Pages on Storefront**: Setting to **Yes** will display this attribute on the product detail page.

- **Used in Product Listing**: Depending on your theme, setting this to **Yes** may allow the attribute to be shown on the category listing pages.

- **Used for Sorting in Product Listing**: Also dependent on your theme, this may allow your attribute to be included as a sorting criteria, much as price, position, and name are used by default.

Creating attribute sets

In order to have attributes available for use when creating a product, it should belong to an **Attribute Set**. Attribute Sets also allow you to make available similar attributes across similar products.

To view the existing Attribute Sets, go to **Stores** | **Attribute Sets**.

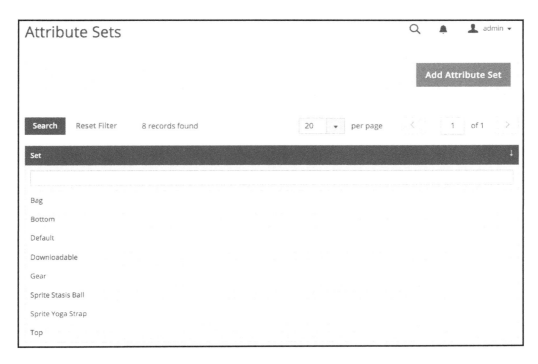

Each existing Attribute Set (the default will appear if you have not created any sets) contains attributes assigned to that set. Let's create a new Attribute Set for our furniture products.

For this exercise, we have already created one new attribute: **fabric**.

1. To begin creating our new Attribute Set, click on **Add Attribute Set**.
2. On the first screen, enter the name of your Attribute Set as you would like it to appear in the backend (your customers will never see Attribute Sets).
3. If you wish, you can base your new set on an existing Attribute Set, which can help reduce your configuration time if an existing set has most of the attributes that you wish to use. For our example, we're going to select **Default**.

Edit Attribute Set Name

Name * Furniture

For internal use

Based On * Default ▾

4. Click on **Save** to advance to the next screen.

5. To add **fabric** to our new Attribute Set, we need to drag it from the **Unassigned Attributes** column on the right, and place it where we want it to appear on the **Product Detail** screen. We can place and move attributes into any order or group within the Attribute Set. A Group is noted by the folders in the **Groups** column.

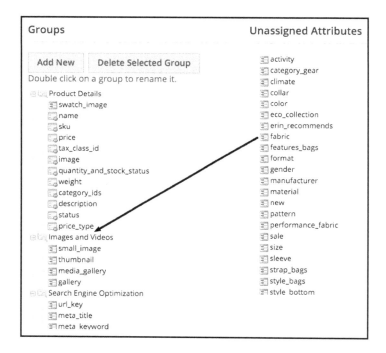

Attributes marked with a Do Not Enter icon cannot be removed from the Attribute Sets. These are required fields for products. All others can be added or removed as needed.

6. If you wish, you can create additional Groups within an Attribute Set by clicking on **Add New** at the top of the Groups column.

7. Click on **Save** to commit your new Attribute Set.

We often create a Group within an Attribute Set to contain special, related attributes. For instance, we could create a group called **Furniture Specifications**, and drag **fabric** and any other new, related attributes into this new Group. This can help focus attention on these special attributes when creating or editing products. The order and groups of attributes have no effect on the frontend presentation, nor will they change any programmatic aspects of Magento 2.

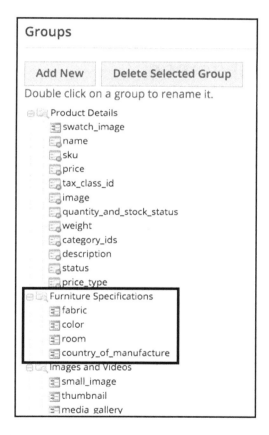

Now that we have created a new Furniture attribute set, we can add additional attributes as needed to help describe our furniture offerings. We can also use this Attribute Set when adding new furniture products so that we have just the attributes related to our needs.

A new and powerful feature of Magento 2 is the ability to add existing attributes within the Product Edit screen. This means that as you create products, you can add the attributes that you need without having to leave your current work. These attributes will also be added to the Attribute Set that you have applied to your current product—this means the attribute will also be added to all products using the same Attribute Set.

Creating products

Now that we've discussed the various Magento product types, let's go over the process of creating a new product in the Magento 2 backend. While there are some differences based on product type, the overall process and options are very similar.

The new product screen

After you go to **Products | Catalog** in the backend, you will see a list of the products in your catalog. In the upper right-hand corner is an orange button, titled **Add Product**. If you click on **Add Product**, you can create a Simple, Configurable, Virtual or Downloadable product. For all types—including the Bundled and Grouped product types—you can also click the button menu (the down arrow on the right side of the button), and choose a specific product type.

The Configurable, Virtual, and Downloadable product types can be created simply by changing the settings within the **Simple Product** detail panel. For example, you can start with a Simple Product, add configurations, and the product type will automatically change to a **Configurable Product** type.

As we go through the product creation process, you'll learn that Magento has really upped their game in Magento 2, making it much easier for you to manage your products. For instance, you can start out by adding all the various t-shirt styles you sell as Simple Products, then go back and create the various size and color variants within those products. In Magento 1.x, you could not change the type of an existing product without first deleting the product, and then re-adding it.

So, let's begin by building a Simple Product, then explore how to create the other Complex product types. For our example, we'll start with a red couch.

Creating a Simple product

To begin, click the **Add Product** button on the **Products | Catalog** screen.

1. Fill in the fields in the **Product Details** section as follows:

   - **Name**: Couch
   - **SKU**: C1234
   - **Price**: 599.99
   - **Tax Class**: Taxable Goods
   - **Quantity**: 100, In Stock
   - **Weight**: Yes, 200 lbs
   - **Categories**: Sofas
   - **Description**: Beautiful, comfortable, and stylish. Our Acme sofa is the perfect couch for formal or casual decór. Durable, yet supple microfiber fabric will last for years.

2. For the **Images and Videos** section, upload the image of a red sofa taken from the Sample Data provided in the earlier Magento versions.

3. Save your product now before proceeding.

4. Next, click on the small down arrow to the right of **Default** at the top of the screen, and type Furniture to select the **Furniture** Attribute Set that you created earlier.

After the screen refreshes, you'll see an additional Attribute Group you created in the sidebar on the left, and any attributes you added to the Attribute Set will be available to you.

5. Enter the following values in the Furniture Specifications panel:

- **Fabric**: microfiber
- **Color**: Red
- **Room**: Living Room
- **Country of Manufacture**: United States

6. Under the **Websites** panel, you need to select **Furniture Website** so that the new product will appear in the **Stores** within the **Furniture Website**.

7. Leave all the other settings as it is for now, and click on **Save**

8. When we view the product on the website, and click on the **More Information** tab, we can see the values of the attributes we have selected.

 For attributes to appear on your product detail screen, as shown in the preceding screenshot, you must set **Visible on Catalog Pages on Storefront** to **Yes** in the Attribute properties.

Creating a Configurable product

Let's say we have our couch available in three colors: red, blue, and green. How would we present all three choices as a single product, yet allow the customer in selecting their desired color?

The simplest way would be to add colors as an option in our Simple Product. However, if we manage inventory separately for each color (let's say we have 100 red, 50 blue, and 30 green sofas in the warehouse), we have to, in essence, create three simple products, and *associate* them to a single Configurable product.

To do that, we have two options: auto-create the associated products from the Configurable product, or create the three individual Simple Products, and then associate them to a new, Configurable product.

First, let's try method one using the couch Simple Product we just created:

1. Open the **Product Edit** screen in the backend, and scroll down to the bottom panel titled **Configurations**. Expand this panel.
2. Click on **Create Configurations**. A new screen will be revealed on the right side of your browser window. A step-by-step navigation will appear at the top to note your progress in creating the associated products.
3. The next step is to select the one or more attributes that will determine the product variants. In our case, we have different sofas based on color. If we have sofas of different colors and fabrics (Three colors and two fabrics would produce six possible combinations), we could select both attributes. For now, select only **Color,** and click on **Next**.
4. Now, we get to select all the different colors we wish to use. We will select **Blue**, **Green**, and **Red** for our example. Click on **Next** to proceed.

5. In *Step 3*, we had some choices to make regarding our images, prices, and quantities. As per our example, select **Apply unique images by attribute to each SKU** for **Images,** as shown in the following screenshot:

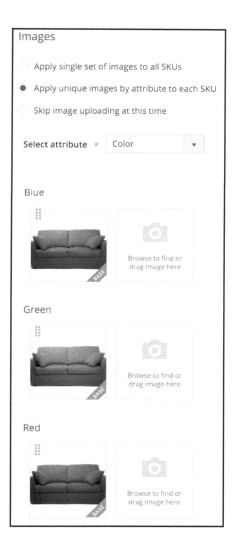

6. Select **Apply single price to all SKUs** for **Price** (all sofas are the same price):

7. Select **Apply unique quantity by attribute to each SKU** for **Quantity**.

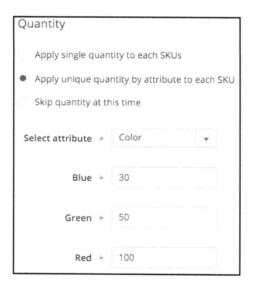

As we make our choices, we have the opportunity to add images and note quantities, since we elected to manage these uniquely for each variant. We will also be able to enter the price common to all sofas (in our case, $599.99). Click on **Next** when you have completed this step.

8. In the final step, you will be able to review your variants to make sure you have them as you wish. When you're satisfied, click on **Generate Products**.

9. The overlay will disappear, and you will see your new variants listed in the
   Configurations panel. Here, you can modify the **Name** and **SKU** for each variant
   to meet your needs. Once you have completed this, click on **Save** to complete the
   process of creating your Configurable product.

Having created the Configurable product, the product on the frontend now displays the
color swatches for each variant (and removes Color from the **More Information** tab
contents). As you click on each swatch, the main image will also change to reflect the image
you uploaded for the particular variant.

In the backend, under **Products | Catalog**, you'll find four products now: the Configurable product and the three new associated Simple Products.

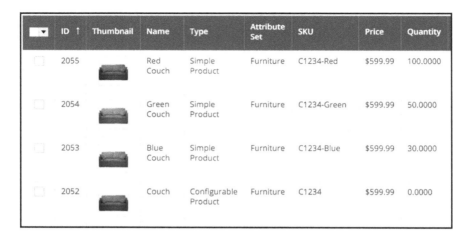

	ID ↑	Thumbnail	Name	Type	Attribute Set	SKU	Price	Quantity
	2055		Red Couch	Simple Product	Furniture	C1234-Red	$599.99	100.0000
	2054		Green Couch	Simple Product	Furniture	C1234-Green	$599.99	50.0000
	2053		Blue Couch	Simple Product	Furniture	C1234-Blue	$599.99	30.0000
	2052		Couch	Configurable Product	Furniture	C1234	$599.99	0.0000

Alternatively, if you already have the Simple Products added to your store, you can create the Configurable product, and add the associated products manually instead of creating them automatically, as we just did.

Creating a Grouped product

If you have a collection of related products, such as yoga straps (included in the Magento 2 Sample Data set), you can present them as a group. Customers can then select the individual items that they want by entering a quantity for each associated product.

To create a Grouped product, choose **Grouped Product** in the **Add Product** drop-down menu, as seen in the following screenshot:

At the bottom of the **Product Details** screen, under **Grouped Products**, you can add products to the group and any default quantity that you wish to set (customers can always override any default).

Grouped Products are not really products at all, but simply a *virtual* grouping of products that you wish to present together.

Creating Bundled product

Bundled products are similar to grouped products, but with some differences. The biggest difference is that you create a bundle of products, which is presented to the customer as one set or bundle. Furthermore, you can configure the product so that the customer can select options of each product, if they wish.

Let's look at the **Sprite Yoga Companion Kit** product provided in the Magento 2 Sample Data. This is a bundle of yoga equipment that has been configured to include four required products: a Stasis Ball, a Foam Yoga Brick, a Yoga Strap, and a Foam Roller. Customers can select larger balls and longer straps. The price of the bundle is automatically calculated based on their selections.

When the customer clicks on **Customize and Add to Cart**, the choices available for the bundle are revealed.

First are the choices for the Statsis Ball, displayed as follows:

As customers select alternative sizes, the total cost of the bundle will adjust accordingly.

Bundled products are created in two steps: creating the options for each bundle component, and then attaching simple products to those options.

 Simple products used in Bundled products cannot have custom options. Remember that, as with all Complex product types, you can only associate Simple or Virtual products. Complex product types cannot be associated with other Complex product types.

Let's build the Sprite Stasis Ball bundle option, as shown, in the **Product Detail** screen to illustrate this two-step process.

1. Under the **Bundle** panel, click on **Create New Option**.
2. For **Option Title**, we'll enter Sprite Stasis Ball.
3. We can allow the customer to make their selection using a drop-down menu, radio buttons, or a checkbox. You should use whatever you feel best communicates the choices to your customers. For our example, we're going to select **Radio Buttons**.
4. Our next step is to click on **Add Products to Option**. We can then use the search tools to find the products that we want to add to this option. In our case, we're going to search for products with **Stasis Ball** in the title and **blue** in the **SKU**. We will check each product that we want to attach to our option, and click on **Add Selected Products**.

ID	↑	Product	SKU	Price	
		Stasis Ball	blue	From	
				To	
	✓	Sprite Stasis Ball 75 cm	24-WG083-blue	$32.00	
	✓	Sprite Stasis Ball 65 cm	24-WG082-blue	$27.00	
	✓	Sprite Stasis Ball 55 cm	24-WG081-blue	$23.00	

Once you have created your options and attached the associated products, you can save your product.

There are lots of possibilities for how you can use Bundled products in Magento. You should experiment, trying various configurations and settings to arrive at the ideal product setup for your needs.

Creating a Downloadable product

In today's digital world, many online retailers offer files that can be purchased and downloaded, such as books, music, and software. Creating a Downloadable product is achieved by attaching the files to the product. Once purchased, the customer will receive a link they can click to download their purchase to their computer.

 Note that many Downloadable products cannot be redeemed on mobile devices. Music, for example, may not always be downloadable and playable on a mobile device by clicking the redemption link. Please experiment and test your offerings so you know how to communicate any restrictions to your customers.

A Downloadable product is created by making two initial selections:

- **Weight**: For the question "Does this have a weight?", you should select **No**.
- **Is this downloadable Product?** (sic): This box is checked to reveal the fields necessary to attach files that define your product.

In the **Downloadable Information** panel, there are two sections:**Links** and **Samples**. The **Links** section allows you to attach files that will be provided to customers once they purchase your products. The **Samples** section will provide linked files for shoppers to download as examples of what they will get when they buy the product. You can also use this section to attach files to promote the product.

When creating a Downloadable product, you have control over the ease of sharing their download link for the customer and the number of times they can download their purchase. While these are not foolproof, they can help restrict the distribution of your digital products.

Creating a Virtual product

A Virtual product is just as it sounds: a product that doesn't actually exist, but can be purchased by the customer. Basically, a Virtual product is one that has no weight, and therefore, cannot be shipped.

What kind of products fall into this type? We've used the Virtual product type for extended warranties, training courses, and hosting packages.

Managing inventory

If you sell actual products, you no doubt have inventory stock. Except in cases where you are having products drop-shipped from a distributor, and have no means of monitoring inventory availability, you need to make sure you have enough inventory on hand to fulfill your orders. Furthermore, you may want to restrict customers' ability to order products that are out of stock-or, alternatively, allow customers to place backorders.

Magento has a host of configurations to help you establish your inventory rules and policies. Most can be overridden at the product level too, giving you even more granular control over your product inventory needs.

You can manage the individual inventory configurations of each product in the **Advanced Inventory** panel under **Advanced Settings**. These settings are very similar to the ones found in the **Stores** | **Configuration** | **Catalog** | **Inventory** panel.

The inventory configurations are covered in Chapter 2, *Settings and Configurations*. Here, let's discuss some additional tools in Magento that can help you manage your inventory.

Low stock notifications

One of the inventory configurations described in Chapter 2, *Settings and Configurations* is that of **Notify for Quantity Below**. This value sets the threshold whereby Magento will send you an e-mail notification if a product's inventory falls below this quantity. This notification will only come once each day for a given product. Using this feature can help you avoid running out of stock.

Product reports

Under the **Reports** menu in your Magento backend are several reports under the **Products** section. Use these reports regularly to help you in monitoring your inventory movements and for planning your stock purchases.

Before using reports, you may need to refresh Magento's statistics under **Reports | Refresh Statistics**.

- **Views**: This report shows the popularity of your products in terms of how often products are viewed by customers. If you have products that are often viewed, but convert to few sales, you may want to evaluate pricing and content for possible improvements to encourage more sales.
- **Bestsellers**: Magento keeps track of the number of times products are sold, and presents a list of these products to show you those which are most commonly purchased.
- **Low Stock**: With this report, you can list the products that fall within a specified stock quantity. This is useful in planning your restocking purchases.
- **Ordered**: The Ordered report shows, for each given period (Day, Month, or Year), the number of each SKU purchased during the specified time span.
- **Downloads**: For Downloadable products, this report shows the number of times any digital file was downloaded by your customers.

Pricing tools

Many times, we're faced with the need to manage special pricing for different customer groups, or based on quantities purchased. Flexibility in pricing can help you meet the needs of your market, and Magento gives you the tools necessary to accommodate those considerations.

Pricing by customer group

In Chapter 4, *Preparing to Sell* we learned how to create customer groups. You may, for instance, wish to offer discounted pricing for your wholesale customers—those who buy from you for resale to their customers. At the same time, you want to sell products at regular retail prices for your regular customers.

By creating a customer group—say Wholesale—and assigning select customers to that group, you can set up specific pricing for a product that will appear to customers who are logged into your store, *and* are assigned to the particular customer group.

Let's use the green couch we created earlier as an example of how to configure pricing for a customer group. If we go to the **Product Detail** screen for this product, and click on **Advanced Pricing** under the **Advanced Settings** menu in the sidebar menu on the left, we see a section called **Tier Price** (we will also refer to this section later when we discuss quantity-based pricing).

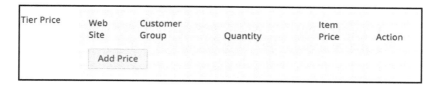

To add pricing for a customer group, click on **Add Price**. If we wish to set the price for this couch—normally selling for $599.99—at $350.00 for our wholesale customer, we might configure this new entry as shown in the following screenshot:

With this configuration, any logged—in customer who belongs to the **Wholesale** customer group will see this couch priced at $350.00 on your store.

Quantity-based pricing

It's probably quite obvious now how you can create quantity-based-or **tiered pricing**-for your products using the same configuration tool. By adding additional pricing tiers and setting a new Quantity value, you can create pricing that changes based on the number of items a customer purchases.

As an example, let's configure the pricing to show a price of $550.00 if a customer buys two-five couches, and a price of $500.00 if they buy six or more. We will apply this to all customer groups.

 Be careful when using tiered pricing and multiple customer groups. Test your configurations carefully.

If we commit this pricing scheme, then when viewing the green couch in the store, we would see the pricing notice seen in the following screenshot:

This notice may help stimulate higher purchased quantities by showing customers how much they can save by buying more!

Autosettings

Before we leave our discussion of product creation and management, we need to discuss a special panel in the **Product Detail** screen: **Autosettings**. This panel is found in the **Advanced Settings** submenu.

Let's go over the particular settings found on this panel. You'll find these can be valuable to your product presentation efforts.

- **Short Description**: The description you enter here will be used in category listings as a brief description of your product. In many themes, this description also appears at the top of the product detail page, usually below the title.
- **Visibility**: You can choose whether you want the product to be visible to customers within category listings (**Catalog**), search results, or not at all. In our couch example, we might not want the individual color couches available outside of the Configurable product; therefore, we would set this field to **Not Visible Individually**.
- **Set Product as New from Date/Set Product as New to Date**: In many themes, you can present new items in special display blocks, or the word New might appear on the product listing. This trigger can be managed by setting from and to dates in these fields. If the current date falls within the dates used here (inclusive), then the product will be considered New.

- **Country of Manufacture**: In our global economy, jurisdictions and regulations often require that a product's country of origin be presented to customers. This is not, by default, a required field, but you can use this to denote the country of origin of that product.
- **Allow Gift Message**: As described in `Chapter 2`, *Settings and Configurations* you can allow customers to add gift messages to products purchased. These messages appear on the packing slip.

Other product selling opportunities

If you've ever shopped online, you've no doubt seen merchants that offer suggested products or present other related items to those you're considering or purchasing. These selling opportunities are available to you as a Magento merchant.

Each of the following product selling features are configured in the **Product Detail** screen under the **Advanced Settings** section. Each one has particular features and purposes.

Related products

Related products are those that you wish to present to customers as additional purchases to include when adding a viewed product to their shopping cart. In other words, if a customer is interested in Product A, they may also want to purchase Product B and Product C at the same time.

As you can see, a customer may select one or more related items to include with the product they are currently viewing.

Upsell products

By contrast, **upsell products** are those to be considered as *alternatives* to the product the customer is viewing. That is, if the customer is interested in Product A, they might instead consider Product B. Not as an additional purchase, but instead of purchasing Product A.

The manner in which related or upsell products are displayed on your store will depend on your theme. Consult your developer if you wish to change how these products are presented.

Cross-sell products

Cross-sell products are presented to your customer on the shopping cart page. For instance, if you want to encourage the purchase of an extended warranty, you could add it as a cross-sell product, and it would be presented in the shopping cart. Your customer can add it to their order directly from the shopping cart.

Summary

We have certainly covered a lot of ground in this chapter. Since the purpose of building and operating a Magento 2 store is to sell products, it is critical that you explore the many ways you can leverage the power of Magento to present and manage your products. We have covered many of the basics, such as:

- Different product types
- Leveraging the power of attributes
- Creating products
- Additional product selling opportunities

You should now dig into the process of adding products, experimenting with various settings to increase your product marketability.

In the next chapter, we turn our attention to how your store looks, and what you can do as a store administrator to modify the look and feel of your store.

6
Themes

The look and feel of your e-commerce store reflects your brand and how you wish to communicate your offerings to your customers. Your product images and description, the words in your content, and your category presentations combine with the framework of a **theme** to create the final display for your site visitors.

While your developer has installed your theme (or themes), you, as the store operator, have the opportunity to specify which theme goes with each of your stores as well as control over special features that add value to how you present your store.

In this chapter, we will cover the following topics:

- Theme hierarchy
- Assigning themes to your store(s)
- Adding branding elements to your store

It's important to note that considerable design modifications are best handled by your Magento developer as today's store layouts require a significant knowledge of HTML, CSS, responsive layout, and the Magento platform architecture. However, Magento 2 has greatly improved its base theme framework, which will make adding new themes or enhancing your site design a much more rewarding and higher performing experience.

Theme hierarchy

One of the best features of Magento is how it is built to support a *fallback* methodology. Let's explore what this means in terms of themes.

Magento 2 is installed with what is called a **Blank theme**. This theme contains all the various pieces of code that will successfully display a Magento store, yet it is without any considerable styling.

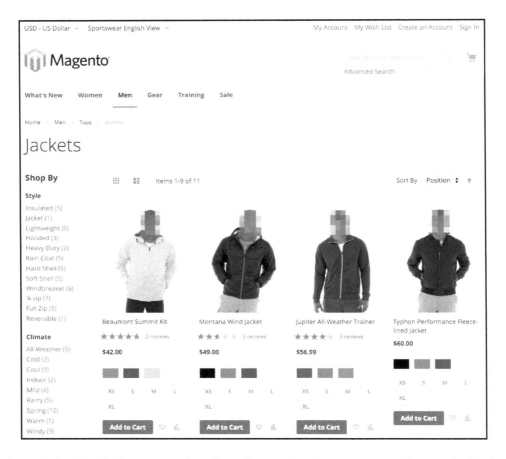

Even though the Blank theme is rather "bare bones," it does a reasonably good job of displaying the features of Magento, and, in all honesty, it could be used as is. However, you would no doubt prefer to have a store that more closely resembles your brand and image.

Using the fallback feature of Magento, a theme developer can create a theme that only contains the enhancements desired. All other aspects of the site presentation would use the Blank theme.

You can compare the Blank theme example shown previously to the **Luma theme** that is included with a Magento 2 sample data installation.

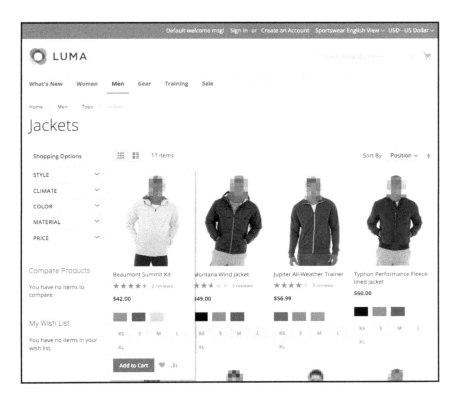

You can immediately notice several design differences:

- The topmost bar is now grey with white text, and the items are shifted to the right
- The filtered navigation on the left-hand side is presented differently
- The **Add to Cart** and other buttons are not shown on the category page until an individual item is hovered over with a mouse
- Various colors, fonts, and spacing are different

The Luma theme was constructed by including files that override the same files in the Blank theme. Where Magento needs a file in order to render a page, it first looks to the Luma theme, and if it is missing, it then takes the file from the Blank theme. This is what is referred to as fallback as Magento "falls back" to the base theme if it cannot find an appropriate file in the assigned theme.

Let's consider a more concrete example to help illustrate the fallback. In the Luma theme files on your server, there are no layout files that control the layout for the Gift Card functionality of the Cart screen. In this case, the Gift Card functionality is controlled by the files in the Blank theme as they do exist in the Blank theme. However, for the catalog page, the Luma theme has a CSS styling file with the same name as the one in the Blank theme. Here, the Luma theme CSS file would take precedence over the Blank theme equivalent.

For your purposes, this means that regardless of any theme you may add to your Magento store, you can rest assured that any theme files that might be missing will not render your store unusable. Magento takes care of you!

Viewing the theme hierarchy

In our example configuration, using the sample data installed with Magento 2, we can view how this hierarchy is represented in your backend. Go to **Content** | **Themes**.

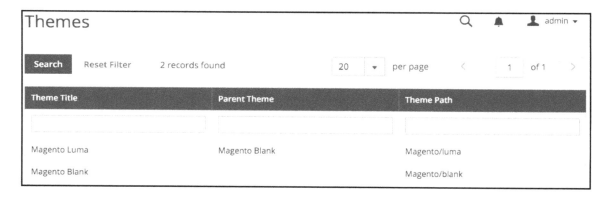

In this installation, there are two themes: **Magento Luma** and **Magento Blank**. If you have other themes installed, you would see those here as well.

Note that Magento Luma has a Parent Theme: Magento Blank. As you learned, the Luma theme falls back to the Blank theme. This is because Blank is the parent of Luma.

Assigning themes

As your developer installs additional themes, you will want to assign themes to each of your stores. For learning purposes, we will assign the Magento Blank theme to our furniture store and the Magento Luma theme to our sportswear store views. As the Luma theme is the one used for most of our store views, we will set it as our default theme for the entire installation. Then, we only have to assign the Blank theme to our furniture store. Perform the following steps:

1. Go to **Stores | Configuration** in your backend.
2. Make sure the **Store View** parameter is set to **Default Config**.
3. Click on **Design** under the **General** side menu panel.
4. Then, expand the **Design Theme** panel.
5. For **Design Theme**, select **Magento Luma**.
6. Click on **Save Config**.

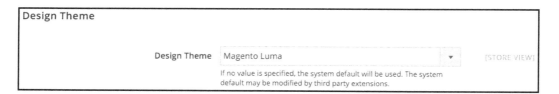

Now, all the stores for which you do *not* specifically set a theme will use the Luma theme. However, for our furniture store, we want to use the simple Blank theme.

Under the **Store View** drop-down menu, select **Furniture English View**.

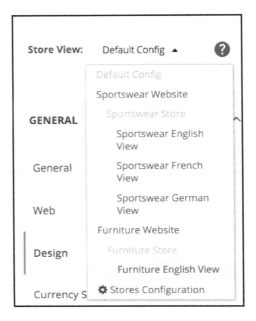

7. In the Design Theme panel, unselect the **Use Website** checkbox.
8. Select **Magento Blank** for **Design Theme**.
9. Finally, click on **Save Config**.

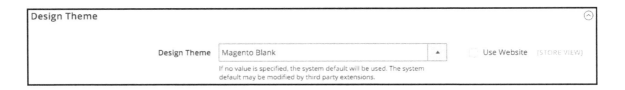

Adding branding elements

Your developer or designer may incorporate your logo and other branding elements into your design. However, if you're using a purchased theme—or one of the default Magento themes—you may want to add these items yourself.

In this section, we will review some of the ways in which you can affect the visual presentation of your store.

Adding your site logo

Using the Luma theme as an example, we will change the default Luma logo to the one we created for Acme Sportswear.

The size you need for your logo is determined by your theme. Some themes constrain the logo size when displayed. For the ideal logo purposes, you should consider the following:

- Size your logo as close to the size of which it will appear on your site. If you upload a huge file, it may be reduced in dimensions for appearance, but your customers will still be downloading a very large file, which can degrade their experience.
- PNG files work best for graphics, yielding sharp, defined edges and a full color palette.
- If you want to have your logo look sharp on retina resolution devices, you should create a logo with width and height dimensions three times that of the displayed size. If you want your logo display size to be 500px wide by 250px high, then your actual logo file size should be 1500px wide by 750px high.

To change our the logo on the Luma theme, the following steps need to be performed:

1. Go to **Stores** | **Configuration** | **General** | **Design** in the backend. This is the same panel in which you assigned your theme.
2. Select the correct Store View in the **Store View** drop-down menu. In our example, we will choose **Sportswear Website** so that the logo we upload will appear on all sportswear Store Views.
3. Expand the **Header** panel.
4. Unselect the **Use Default** checkboxes beside the fields you want to change.
5. For **Logo Image**, click on **Choose File** and select the logo file you created from your computer.
6. If your theme allows, you can set the width and height you wish to display your logo. Enter the number of pixels, but you do not have to enter "px" or "pixels".

7. You should also enter a **Logo Image Alt** value. This is the hidden text that describes your image file. It is also used by web page "readers" to assist sight-impaired visitors. In this case, we would enter `Acme Sportswear Logo`.

8. We can also use this opportunity to update the **Welcome Text** message that appears at the top of our site theme.

9. Finally, click on **Save Config**.

We can now take a look at how our changes updated the frontend design of the site.

Adding your logo to your e-mails

You can also add your custom logo to your outgoing e-mails on the same configuration panel. Perform the following steps:

1. Reveal the **Emails** panel.
2. Select your logo file for **Logo Image**.
3. Next, enter a **Logo Image Alt** value as you did for your site logo.
4. Set the **Logo Width** and **Logo Height** sizes to display on your e-mail.
5. If your theme allows for alternative Header and Footer templates, you can also choose them here.

6. Click on **Save Config**.

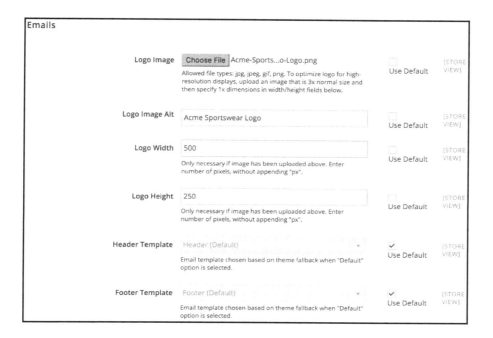

Adding your logo to sales documents

In Magento, you have the opportunity to display orders, invoices, credit memos, and other sales transactions as PDFs or in the HTML format (that is, a web page). You should add your logo to these outputs as well.

For PDF print-outs, you need to create a 200×50 pixel version of your logo. As with most other configurations, you can upload different logos for different Website and Store entities.

1. Go to **Stores | Configuration | Sales | Sales** in your backend.
2. Expand the **Invoice and Packing Slid Design** panel.
3. Choose your PDF logo file for **Logo for PDF Print-outs**.
4. Choose your file for **Logo for HTML Print View**.
5. Fill in the address you wish to have displayed on these documents.
6. Finally, click on **Save Config**.

Third-party themes

Many modern themes built for Magento by some of the more ingenious theme developers add configuration panels to your Magento store backend. These configurations allow you more choices in terms of fonts, colors, and layout.

If you've ever shopped for a Magento theme, you must have found many that have great-looking demos. Some are even specific to different verticals, such as apparel, furniture, or electronics.

Based on our experience, it's best to find a theme that is not specific to a particular product type but rather provides you with a solid foundation to create your own brand design. When analyzing theme possibilities, look for themes:

- With the kind of customizations you need
- That support Magento best practices for theme design, honoring Magento's fallback methodology
- That allow customization for different devices, such as desktops, tablets, and mobiles
- That provide support and regular updates to address any bugs

Summary

The design of your Magento store depends a lot on how your developer configures your installation, including themes. By understanding how themes work in Magento, you can better communicate your needs to your developer as well as properly assign themes to your stores.

Take the time necessary to explore the design and layout options available to you as the store owner. You certainly want your customers to experience your brand as you desire.

In the next chapter, we will work on the content that compliments your brand design as well as ways to improve your search engine visibility.

7
Content and SEO

Optimizing the presentation of products to your online customers is undoubtedly a very important key to your e-tailing success. Your branded theme design is certain to communicate your value proposition. However, it's not yet time to rest. There are still some important core features for which we need to invest time and creativity.

The nonproduct content of your site can often be as important as the products you sell. Customers need to understand your business, your policies, and how to purchase.

Also, if you want customers to find your online store in the first place, you need to get your store noticed by the search engines. Your search engine listings need to also be inspiring to shoppers so that they will click through to your store. **Search engine optimization** (**SEO**) will be one of your ongoing tasks, but it is one that can pay huge dividends if properly managed.

In this chapter, we will:

- Discuss how to manage the static content pages of your site
- Discover the use of blocks and widgets
- Explore the metafields available for SEO
- List hints to improve your search engine visibility

Set aside some time each week to review and enhance your store's content and SEO, and you'll no doubt see continued improvement in traffic and conversions.

Cache

So that Magento can serve your web pages and content as fast as possible, temporary copies of various components are combined and stored on your server. Once a web page is created by Magento, a finished copy can be served from the cached until the cached either "expires" or a change is made to the page. By serving your site from cache, your customers can see your site faster, which leads to a more enjoyable experience.

As you work with content pages, blocks, and widgets, you may need to flush your cache after saving your changes in order to view your updates on the store's frontend. To flush your Magento cache, go to **System | Cache** Management and click on **Flush Magento Cache**.

In some cases, you may need to flush the additional caches, but usually, flushing the general Magento cache is enough.

Managing CMS pages

Most modern platforms, whether for e-commerce or not, have some function to manage *static pages*, which are the unchanging and nonproduct related pages. This feature is called **Content Management System** (**CMS**). While many don't immediately associate e-commerce with CMS, the ability to manage the static pages of your site is just as important as the ability to manage the products you offer. For this reason, Magento 2 has a fairly robust CMS capability.

In most online stores, you will find static pages used for:

- Returns policy
- About the company
- Store locations
- Terms and conditions
- Privacy policy
- Frequently asked questions
- Support
- Company history
- Leadership profiles

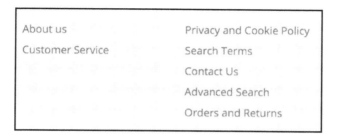

Of course, not all stores have all these pages.

The kinds of pages you add to your store should be considered as important chance to communicate your brand's value, experience, and trustworthiness to your customers. Even a "dry" page such as your site terms and conditions provides a sense of propriety and professionalism to your customers, as well as informs them of the specific considerations that may be important to their decision-making process.

Magento's content pages

In Magento 1, static pages were referred to as CMS pages. In Magento 2, all content-related components, including theme design (refer to `Chapter 6`, *Themes*) are put under the **Content** menu:

In an initial Magento 2 installation, there are a few necessary and useful content pages created:

	ID ↓	Title	URL Key	Layout	Store View	Status
	1	404 Not Found	no-route	2 columns with right bar	All Store Views	Enabled
	2	Home Page	home	1 column	All Store Views	Enabled
	3	Enable Cookies	enable-cookies	1 column	All Store Views	Enabled
	4	Privacy Policy	privacy-policy-cookie-restriction-mode	1 column	All Store Views	Enabled
	5	About us	about-us	1 column	All Store Views	Enabled
	6	Customer Service	customer-service	1 column	All Store Views	Enabled

While it's not absolutely necessary that you keep these pages enabled, it's generally best practice in e-commerce to use these core pages. Take a look at the following:

- **404 Not Found**: This page is displayed to visitors who land on a nonexisting page on your site. For example, you might have a product that is discontinued and that you no longer wish to keep visible to customers. However, a search engine, blog, or other website may have a link to this product. If a customer clicks on this link and comes to your site, then as the item is no longer visible, they would be shown this page. A 404 error is *webspeak* for missing page. You can provide branded content to visitors who try to access a missing page. Without this page, such a visitor would simply see a stark 404 Error page provided by your web server, and it's neither appealing nor branded.
- **Home Page**: Obviously, this is the home page for your site. The content and design elements that appear at the core of your home page are managed on this page.
- **Enable Cookies**: In order for your store's shopping cart, login, and other features to work properly, a customer's web browser must allow **cookies** to be used. If Magento detects that cookies cannot be used on a customer's browser, they will see the content of this page. You can use this page to help customers understand cookies and how to activate them on their browser.

- **Privacy Policy**: Online privacy and the sharing of information is increasingly important to consumers. Furthermore, Google considers sites that have a comprehensive privacy policy on their site favorably. It's just good business sense! The default Magento privacy policy content is a great boilerplate with which to construct your own policy.
- **About Us**: Would you hand over your hard-earned money to someone you didn't trust? There are lots of ways to demonstrate your good faith and reputation on your site, and the About Us page is one ideal place to start. Give your shoppers a sense of your mission, leadership team, and history.
- **Customer Service**: You can create other service-related pages (for example, Returns Policy, FAQs, and so on). At least, you should have a page that discusses your customer service policies. Magento provides this page with the initial installation because any reputable online store should make their service policies available to online shoppers.

We suspect that you're already thinking of other pages you wish to include on your site. Pages are relatively easy to construct, and with help from your developer, you can include additional layouts and features, allowing you to create some quite customized presentations.

Creating a CMS page

Let's add a new page to our site calledCare Instructions. We want to provide information to our apparel site customers on the proper techniques of washing the clothing items they purchase from Acme Sportswear. Perform the following steps:

1. Go to **Content** | **Pages** in the Magento 2 backend.
2. Click on **Add New Page**.

The first panel is titled **Page Information**.

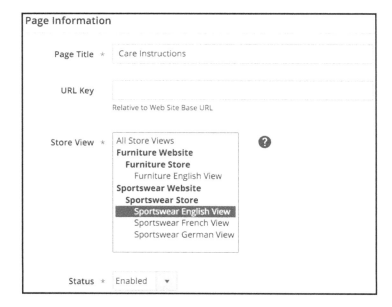

As shown, we entered the initial information for our new page. Magento will create a URL Key once the new page is saved. However, you can enter the URL Key here, just as you learned when creating products in `Chapter 5`, *Products*. URL Key is the actual name used in the URL to access your page—for example, `http://www.acmesportswear.com/care-instructions.html`. If you want another URL Key value, you can enter it here.

 If you build different pages for *different Store Views*, they can each use the same URL Key value. However, if you try to use the same URL Key value for two pages that are both assigned to the same Store View, you will get an error.

The next panel in the new product screen is **Content**. It is in this panel that you can create the words, images, and so on, that will appear in the main content portion of your new page.

The **WYSIWYG editor** gives you a lot of great tools to help build your page content. You can easily insert images, videos, tables, and other styled content.

The content heading appears at the top of your page. It is displayed within an `<h1>` tag.

If you're not familiar with HTML heading tags—or other HTML elements—you should consider enlisting the assistance of an experienced web content editor. The proper use of headings, styles, and other HTML elements can have an effect on how well your content is indexed by Google.

The third panel in the menu to the left is labeled **Design**. Based on your theme, you can change the layout of the page to a one-, two-, or three-column display. You can also specify a special theme design (as described in `Chapter 6`, *Themes*). There are additional **XML** statements that can be inserted, which will affect your display. The use of XML in this instance should be discussed with your Magento developer.

The last panel is **Meta Data**. Keep this in mind for when we discuss metainformation later in this chapter.

Once saved, we can view our new page by going to the URL path we created for this page:

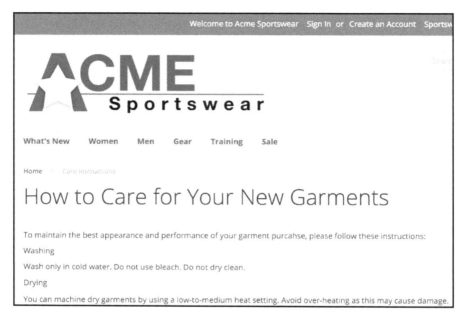

Now, we're pretty sure you're now wondering about how you will add a link to the new page to your site. One easy way is to edit a *block* that contains links to pages within your site. Read on!

Using blocks and widgets

Blocks are sections of content that are specified by your theme to appear in various places throughout your site. Blocks can be placed on all pages, some pages, product pages, category pages, or in special, designated spots.

In addition to block locations that are configured within your theme, blocks can be inserted into various areas and pages within your site using **widgets**, which we will explore just a bit later in this section.

To view all the blocks on your site, go to **Content | Blocks**. If you installed the Magento 2 sample data, you'll see as many as 18 blocks. By their names, you can probably figure out where they appear on your site. Take a look at the table in the following screenshot:

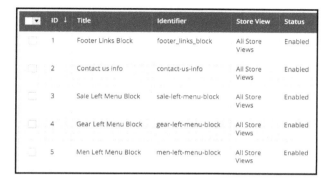

To understand how blocks work—and to add our *Care Instructions* page link—click on the **Select** drop-down menu to the far right of the first block, **Footer Links Block**, and click on **Edit**.

This block contains the information that appears in the bottom footer of all our sites:

We want to add our *Care Instructions* link to this block. Now, this is where things get just a tad complex, so read through this process carefully as it applies any time you wish to add a page link from your site to a block. We will explain three different methods of accomplishing the same result. The method you choose is up to your own preference.

Adding a link using WYSIWYG

We can add a link using the WYSIWIG editor, or we could change the view to HTML mode and edit the actual HTML code. Let's do this using the WYSIWYG editor first.

In the editor space, add the link name as you wish it to appear on the frontend by adding another bullet row below the **Customer Service** label. You can, of course, insert your new link anywhere in the list.

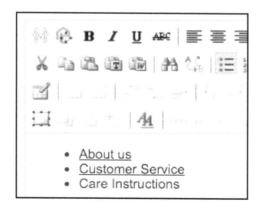

To create the link, select the title you just entered and click on the *link* icon in the menu toolbar. A *modal* dialogue will appear for you to enter your link URL.

Magento provides a library of variables that can be used to dynamically insert values and content where appropriate. Usually, these variables are used by your developer as they modify various templates and themes. However, in this case, the use of a **system variable** to insert the Store URL is worth learning for our purposes.

The **Store URL variable** is inserted when used in the format `{{store url=URL_Key}}`, where `URL_Key` is the URL Key value for the page, category, or product you wish to access.

Therefore, for our new page, we will insert `{{store url=care-instructions}}` into **Link URL**. Add a **Title** value for your link so that it will appear when your customer hovers over the link and help describe the link to search engines.

 In most Magento help guides, the format to enter a Store URL variable is `{{store url="URL_Key"}}`, with quotes (") around the URL Key value. However, we must leave out the quotes when using this variable within the link dialogue box. It's quite possible to use the Store URL variable without quotes elsewhere too. This behavior does not apply when adding links using HTML (refer to the next section).

Once you click on **Import**, the text will be linked. If you look at the frontend of your website, you will see a new link in the footer:

About us

Customer Service

Care Instructions

 As you'll notice, if you select a link in WYSIWYG and click on the link icon, the URL that shows in the dialogue field is a very long, encrypted string. This is due to the way Magento stores link references. You can edit the link by replacing it with what you prefer as the link, but you may find building and managing links much easier using HTML than the WYSIWYG view.

Adding a links using HTML

The method of adding a link using the Store URL variable is the same if you work in the HTML view. The key, of course, is knowing how to properly code an HTML link.

In the block screen, click on **Show/Hide Editor** to reveal the underlying HTML for this block. Take a look at the following code:

```
<ul class="footer links">
  <li class="nav item"><a href="{{store url="about-us"}}">About
  us</a></li>
  <li class="nav item"><a href="{{store url="customer-
  service"}}">Customer Service</a></li>
  <li class="nav item"><a title="How to care for your new garment
  purchases." href="{{store%20url=care-instructions}}">Care
  Instructions</a></li>
</ul>
```

You'll notice that the link you created for the Care Instructions page is slightly different from the other links in the block. This is due to the manner in which the link dialogue saves your entry.

You can also use `{{store url="care-instructions"}}` for the link—in HTML view only—and achieve the same results.

Adding a page link using a widget

If you're hesitant about using the Store URL variable or coding in HTML, you can use one additional technique to insert a link: the **CMS widget**. In fact, as you explore this method, you'll find that it can also be used to insert:

- A CMS page link
- A CMS block
- A link to a category listing
- A link to a product page
- A list of new products
- A list of products belonging to a specific category
- A form for customers to use to look up orders and/or request a return
- A list of the recently compared products
- A list of the recently viewed products

For our example, we want to insert a link to a CMS page. In the WYSIWYG view (you can also use the HTML view), click on the Widget icon in the upper menu bar.

A panel will open from the right-hand side of your screen. For **Widget Type**, select **CMS Page Link**. Then, additional fields will appear.

- **Anchor Custom Text**: Enter what you wish the link to read to your customer. In our case, we would enter `Care Instructions`.
- **Anchor Custom Title**: Enter the hidden title that you wish to use to describe the link to search engines and have displayed to customers if they hover over the link with their mouse.

- **Template**: If you wish to insert the link on a line by itself, select **CMS Page Link Block Template**. If the link is to appear within a paragraph of text, choose **CMS Page Link Inline Template**.
- **CMS Page**: Click on **Select Page...** to choose the page that you want to link.

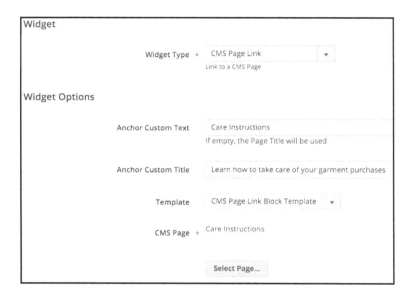

After you insert the widget, it will appear in your WYSIWYG editor as an icon labeled **page link**. If you want to edit the link, simply double-click on the icon to open the Widget panel.

 You may find that using a widget adds more HTML to the actual code. In our example case, the link title is enclosed by a `<span>` tag. Your site's CSS styling may add more styling to this added HTML code, which may affect your site's appearance. If you need help in making CSS adjustments, call upon your Magento developer or designer.

Using variables

The Store URL variable is only one of the many available for use in Magento 2. Most are only truly useful to your developer, but within the CMS page and block editors, you do have access to a list of standard variables that *dynamically* insert information into your content, which are as follows:

- **Base Unsecure URL**
- **Base Secure URL**
- **General Contact Name**
- **General Contact Email**
- **Sales Representative Contact Name**
- **Sales Representative Contact Email**
- **Custom1 Contact Name**
- **Custom1 Contact Email**
- **Custom2 Contact Name**
- **Custom2 Contact Email**
- **Store Name**
- **Store Phone Number**
- **Store Hours**
- **Country**
- **Region/State**
- **Zip/Postal Code**
- **City**
- **Street Address 1**
- **Street Address 2**

Let's say we want to include the name and store hours of our business in the same footer block that we were editing. Perform the following steps:

1. Click on the WYSIWYG editor where you wish to insert your new text and variables.
2. Insert any text you wish.
3. Then, place your cursor where you wish to insert a variable.

4. Click on the Variable icon in the WYSIWYG editor menu:

5. Click on the variable you wish to insert. In our case, we will click on **Store Name** and **Store Hours**. Magento will insert the proper variable code into your text.

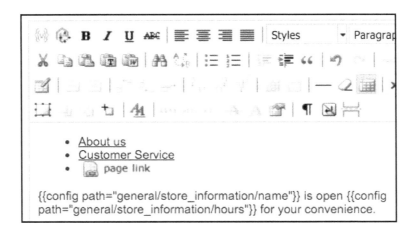

After saving the block, you will see on your site that the actual saved information for Store Name and Store Hours (refer to `Chapter 2`, *Settings and Configurations*) is inserted into its proper place:

About us

Customer Service

Care Instructions

Acme Enterprises is open 10a - 7p CT for your convenience.

Creating your own variables

This is one of the least-known features of Magento administration, and yet it can be powerful in reducing the need to edit changes in multiple places on your site. In fact, **custom variables** can be used not only in pages and blocks but also in **e-mail templates**.

As an example, let's say you'd like to add to your footer message the days on which you are closed, but you'd like to use a variable just in case you decide later to change the days on which you are not open. The following are the steps to perform:

1. Go to **System | Custom Variables** in your store backend.
2. Click on **Add New Variable**.

- **Variable Code**: Enter a code for your variable using only lowercase letters, numbers, and underscore (_). This code is used by Magento's programming to reference your variable.
- **Variable Name**: Enter a name that will appear in the list of variables.
- **Variable HTML Value**: If you wish to insert HTML code as part of the variable value, enter it in this space.
- **Variable Plain Value**: If you do not need any HTML code, enter the value of the variable in this field.

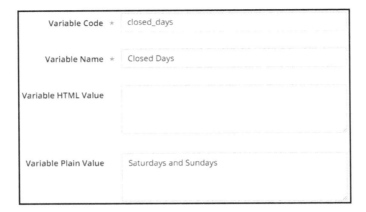

Now, you can return to your footer block and insert your new variable just as you inserted the variables for Store Name and Store Hours. Run the following code:

```
{{config path="general/store_information/name"}} is open {{config
path="general/store_information/hours"}} for your convenience. We are
closed on {{customVar code=closed_days}}.
```

With these variables inserted, your site footer now shows the added variable value:

Custom variables can be handy to manage content that you may wish to edit from time to time, and that needs to be displayed in multiple places, such as:

- The estimated shipping time
- Credit cards and payment methods accepted
- Store pick-up hours
- Alternate phone numbers
- Customer service hours and/or phone number

If any of these need updating on your site, you simply need to change the value of the custom variable.

Using widgets to insert content onto the site pages

The widgets we used in the editing blocks allowed us to insert dynamic links to blocks and pages. However, widgets can also be used to insert dynamic content into multiple pages and theme locations such as products, categories, footers, and so on. In fact, the footer links block we were editing is inserted into the theme's footer *content area* using a widget.

Let's take a look at this particular widget to see how it is configured. Go to **Content | Widgets** and click on the **Footer Links** widget shown in the list.

The first panel, **Storefront Properties**, configures where the widget displays its contents. The **Type** and **Design Package/Theme** values are set when the widget is created and cannot be changed later (although the widget can be deleted and re-created).

You can also assign the widget to appear in only certain Store Views and control the order in which it may appear if other widgets are also assigned to the same layout section.

The **Layout Updates** section is where much of the magic of widgets comes in. You can assign a widget to appear on all pages, certain pages, or certain types of pages (or any combination thereof!).

For categories and products, you can also specify specific categories and products. For instance, you could create a widget that would insert a block of content to appear only on the Furniture category page.

In this particular example, this widget inserts a CMS block (our footer links) into a **container** called **CMS Footer Links**. Depending on your theme, you can have many different containers to choose from, such as in the Luma theme used in our demo store.

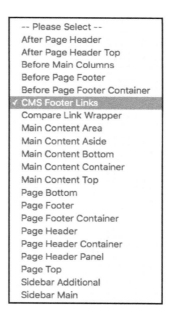

By clicking on **Add Layout Update**, you can also insert the widget content into other containers in your site.

Finally, the **Widget Options** panel allows you to select the block, link, and so on that your widget will insert. This depends on the type of widget you create.

Widgets can be very powerful tools, especially when combined with blocks. We've seen many situations where even experienced developers programmed block insertions instead of using the simple widget tools in Magento. Get to know blocks and widgets, and we're certain you'll come up with some very creative ways of adding true value to your brand and customer experience.

SEO meta fields

SEO is both important and often misunderstood. There's probably as much misinformation on the Internet about SEO as there is good, solid advice.

While we don't have the opportunity or space to go into great detail about SEO in this book, we can help you establish good practices that can reap great rewards in terms of increasing your search engine visibility and helping online shoppers know what you're offering.

Meta fields are bits of data that are stored in the HTML code of a web page. Customers can't see this code as it's not displayed by the browser. However, search engines can see this data (in fact, they can see everything "under the hood"). Google, Bing, and others use this metadata in conjunction with many other analyzed items on your page to determine how to present your site to search users, including the rank and content.

Using meta fields for search engine visibility

It begins with a basic understanding of how search engines use meta fields, particularly Google as Google provides you with most of your search-engine-referred traffic.

Take a look at this Google search result:

> Yves Delorme Caribbean Lt. Down Comforters - Everett Stunz
> https://www.everettstunz.com/**caribbean-lt-comforter** ▾
> **Yves Delorme Caribbean Lt**. Down **Comforters**: 100% Egyptian cotton Batiste, TC
> 305, with sateen piping. Fill power 700. White goose down (min. 90%).

The title **Yves Delorme Caribbean Lt. Down Comforters – Everett Stunz** is taken from the **Title** field of the product page, unless a value is used in the **Meta Title** field of the product in Magento. If so, Google would use the **Meta Title** value instead.

 The URL of the page is, of course, the actual link to the product page. As we described in `Chapter 2`, *Settings and Configurations*, the use of Canonical URLs is important as it gives Google one link to the product, even though, as in this case, the product is also accessible by going to `http s://www.everettstunz.com/brand/yves-delorme-luxury-french -linen/caribbean-lt-comforter` and `https://www.everettstunz. com/down/comforters/caribbean-lt-comforter`.

Without the use of Canonical URLs, Google would see this as three different pages, each with the exact same content. Google is known to *penalize* sites that contain duplicate content by decreasing their rank position.

Finally, the description part of the listing comes first from any existing **Meta Description** field. If none exists, Google will attempt to construct a meaningful description from the content of the page. Using a **Meta Description** field, you can control how the product is described in search engines.

Meta fields in Magento

In `Chapter 2`, *Settings and Configurations*, we talked about the use of **Product Fields Auto-Generation**—that is, the use of variables to automatically construct meta values for your products. While this is certainly a fast way of populating meta fields in products, it's also important to attend to the meta fields for CMS pages and categories. Also, there may be certain products that you want to insert special titles and descriptions into to enhance their search engine presentation.

Do not undervalue the efforts you take to improve your site's SEO, as much of your traffic comes from search engines. However, also be aware of SEO scams and bogus offers from so-called SEO experts. If anyone says they can guarantee you first page position, they are scammers. No one can guarantee first page search results. This position comes from paying careful attention to your meta information, product, and page content and really knowing your customers and your products. There are no shortcuts, but there are "best practices".

The SEO checklist

As you prepare your site for launch—and beyond launch—take the time to address each important SEO feature in Magento. Take a look at this checklist:

- **Meta title fields**: Enter a title no longer than 50-60 characters. Any more will be truncated when displayed in search results. Including your company name is nice but not critical; the customer is looking for a specific product. Use your company's name on the home page meta title, and they'll find you if they search for your brand. If customers shop by SKU, include the SKU or part number in the title.

- **Meta description fields**: Describe your product in 150 characters or less. Use action verbs and strong adjectives, such as `Save 20% on Yoga gear today! Top quality, 100% guarantee, and free shipping` or `Premium 48-inch Yoga ball. Great durability,hypoallergenic material. Guaranteed. Free shipping.`

- **Meta keywords**: Meta keywords are no longer given any ranking weight by search engines. However, it doesn't hurt to include at least the name of the product as a clue for search engines.

- **Canonical URLs**: Make sure to activate **Canonical Link Meta Tags** under **Stores | Configuration | Catalog | Catalog | Search Engine Optimization**. This will reduce any potential duplicate content penalties.

- **XML Sitemap**: Configure and activate your XML sitemap in **Stores | Configuration | Catalog | XML Sitemap**. Search engines use this to learn the hierarchy of your site and to make sure they visit all the pages in your store. Don't forget to change the value of **Enable Submission to Robots.txt** to **Yes**.

- **Category and Product Descriptions**: Don't be shy about describing your products. Use 300 words or more to really sell your product. Category descriptions can also help by informing the search engines about your categories, noting the brands offered, and generally inspiring customers to carefully consider your product offerings.

 Magento 2 also includes a number of SEO features, such as rich snippets. These are the hidden bits of data that provide Google et al with specific information about your products in a format that they understand. Price, availability, SKU, and more are easily read by the search engines regardless of how this information is or is not presented to your customers.

Summary

It's been long said that "content is king." While this is usually aimed at blogs and information sites, it is equally true for e-commerce sites.

There's no argument that product information and accuracy is important for sales. However, the value of your brand, your company, and your customer satisfaction comes from much more than the display of an item on your store. The difference between online success and mediocrity can often be attributed to the quality of content on a site.

In this chapter, you learned how to use the various tools of Magento 2 to build and manage content. We also explored how Magento can assist you in search engine optimization. Now, you can leverage these to maximize your visibility to customers.

Let's now turn our attention to learning about other Magento tools that you can use to actively promote your site to and communicate with your customers.

8
Promotions and Communication

If you've been working on your Magento website while going through this book, you've accomplished quite a lot! In fact, you may already have launched your new store as you have it configured, designed, populated with products, and fleshed out with static content.

However, if you've ever been in retail before, you know that successful selling is more than offering products. As with most business endeavors, the more you put into your online selling efforts, the more you'll get back.

In this chapter, we want to:

- Create store promotions and discounts
- Manage newsletter subscriptions
- Edit transactional e-mails

These are all tools that can help stimulate sales and increase return visits from your customers.

Store promotions

If you are already familiar with online discount codes, especially if you do any online shopping yourself, you will know that discount codes can be distributed and used as *virtual coupons* to entice customers to buy products and receive specials savings. In Magento 2, these are referred to as **Cart Price Rules**.

However, in Magento, you can also configure **automatic price discounts** that are applied to products meeting certain criteria. These types of discounts are called **Catalog Price Rules**.

Creating Cart Price Rules

Magento has some very powerful and flexible tools to create discounts that can be applied once the customer reaches the shopping cart part of their visit. In fact, we find it difficult to identify a single discount scenario that we cannot accommodate in Magento.

BOGO Offers

The one promotion situation that is not handled natively by Magento 2 is the **Buy-One-Get-One** (**BOGO**) offer. Magento promotions are designed to discount cart products and shipping, not to add new products to a cart. You can, however, create a BOGO offer either by using a third-party extension or a product bundle to automatically add another product to an existing product. The latter method is perhaps not as smooth as having a product added to the cart based on the selection of a qualifying product, but it can work in a pinch.

A third method, although it requires considerable trust in that the customer will understand what is needed, is to ask customers to place the free product into their cart. You can then create the price rule to discount the free product 100%. The challenge, of course, is having customers understand that they have to place both the qualifying product and the free product into their shopping cart.

The one exception is that you can specify a number of free items as long as the free items have the same SKU as the qualifying item. That is, you can allow such a rule as buy three of product X and get the fourth one free. This can be specified in the **Actions** panel (described later in this section).

The key features of Cart Price Rules of which you should be aware are as follows:

- You can create rules for any or all of your Website entities. Rules apply to all Store Views within a Website entity.
- You can allow discounts for only the selected customer groups. You could offer coupons to wholesalers, for instance, that cannot be used for retail customers.
- You do not have to use a coupon code. Your rules can be applied automatically as long as the shopping cart meets the required criteria.
- You can limit the number of times a coupon is used. Alternatively, you can allow a coupon code to be used multiple times by a given customer.

- Product attributes can be used as criteria. As noted in `Chapter 5`, *Products*, a product attribute can be configured so that you can apply a discount based on the value of this attribute within one or more products in the customer's shopping cart.
- You can apply the discount to the entire cart or to only select products in the cart. For instance, if, you give a 20% discount to shirts but customers put other types of products in their cart, you can configure the discount so that it deducts 20% from the price of the shirts in the cart and no other product.
- Magento can generate coupon codes. Some e-commerce systems require that you contrive the coupon codes you wish to use. In Magento, you have the ability to generate and manage as many codes as you need.

> We have worked with clients that have millions of generated coupon codes. While so many codes may require more horsepower for your server, Magento has no problem storing and using a very large number of codes.

Let's use a specific example to take a look at how to create a Cart Price Rule:

- We'll consider retail customers only and assume that we have 100 customers on our newsletter list
- We'll have unique coupon codes for each user (we'll e-mail them to the existing customers)
- Customer must buy women's tops worth $100 or more or three or more of any women's apparel items
- A discount will give 20% off women's apparel
- The discount will also provide free ground shipping
- The coupon can only be used once per customer
- The coupon is only active starting on April 1, 2016, and will expire on August 31, 2016.
- The coupon cannot be combined with any other discounts.

The process of building our rule will follow these steps:

1. Add the new rule.
2. Define the rule's conditions.
3. Define the rule's actions.
4. Modify the rule's labels.
5. Generate coupon codes (if needed).
6. Test the rule.

Adding the new rule

To begin building our Cart Price Rule, go to **Marketing** I **Cart Price Rules** in your Magento 2 backend and click on **Add New Rule**.

The **Rule Information** panel for our new rule has several fields to use to set up the rule, which are:

- **Rule Name**: Enter Free Shipping & 20% off Women's Apparel as the name of your rule. This will be shown in your list of rules.

Rule Name ⋆	Free Shipping & 20% off Women's Apparel

- **Description**: You can use this field to more fully describe the rule. In our example, we will enter the coupon specifics we outlined for this example.

Description	• Retail customers only. We'll assume we have 100 customers on our newsletter list. • Unique coupon codes for each user (we'll be email them to existing customers). • Customer must be $100 or more of women's tops or 3 or more of any women's apparel items. • Discount gives 20% off any women's apparel products. • Discount also provides free ground shipping. • Coupon can only be used once per customer. • Coupon is only active starting on April 1, 2016 and expiring on August 31, 2016. • Coupon cannot be combined with any other discounts.

- **Status**: Select **Active** when you wish for the coupon to be available for use.
- **Websites**: Select **Sportswear Website**, as our example rule only applies to the products purchased in this store. You can select any number (or all) of the Website entities shown. Our selection also means that visitors to all the three Sportswear Store Views (English, French, and German) can use the code.

- **Customer Groups**: As we only want our coupon to be used by retail customers, we will select **NOT LOGGED IN** and **General**. If we only wanted the logged-in retail customers, we would have only selected General.

- **Coupon**: We will use a coupon code, so select **Specific Coupon**.
- **Coupon Code**: Our goal is to create 100 unique codes to distribute. This may help us track the code usage by customer. Also, it will allow us to restrict the usage of the code to only one use as we will be distributing to customers that are not logged in. Instead of entering a specific coupon code, select the box labeled**Use Auto Generation**. (We will manage the generation of code in a moment.)
- **Uses per Coupon**: Enter 1, as we want to only allow a customer to use the code once before expiring.
- **Uses per Customer**: This value only applies to logged-in customers. We will also enter 1 in this field.

 Entering zero in either of the "Uses" fields allows unlimited use of a coupon.

- **From/To**: These are the first and last dates on which the coupon can be used. If you leave **To** blank, the coupon will be immediately available (if *Active*); if **From** is blank, the coupon code will never expire. Using the calendar popup (click on the small icon to the right), choose April 1, 2016 for **To** and August 31, 2016 for **From**.

- **Priority**: If you have more than one active rule, they will be applied in an order based on this field. The order is numeric and descending, with 1 being the highest priority.
- **Public In RSS Feed**: If you want to publicize your discount in your store's RSS field, set this to **Yes**. As ours requires a specific coupon code and we wish to limit it to the known newsletter subscribers, we will select **No** for this field.

As with all multipanel screens in Magento, it's probably a good idea to click on **Save and Continue Edit** after you complete each panel… Just in case!

Defining the rule's conditions

A rule's conditions can be considered as minimum requirements. In other words, this is what is necessary regarding a customer's shopping cart for the rule to be valid.

In our example, a coupon code can only be used if the shopping cart contains $100 or more of women's tops or three or more women's apparel items. To create this condition, go to the **Conditions** panel.

If we leave this panel blank (that is, if we do not add any conditions), then the coupon code will be valid for any product present in the shopping cart and for any amount.

As we have two conditions, either of which are valid, click on **ALL** in **If ALL of these conditions are TRUE**. It will allow you to select **ANY**, which creates an "or" condition.

Pay attention when you use nested conditions as the **ALL/ANY** option applies to only the top-level conditions. You can use **Condition Combinations** to create nested and/or conditions.

Our first condition will test whether the customer has $100 or more of women's tops in their shopping cart.

1. Click on the green + icon to create your first condition.
2. In the drop-down menu, select the **Products** subselection. We will create a rule that will apply to only a particular selection of qualifying products.
3. Click on the words **total quantity** and select **total amount**.
4. Click on the word **is** and select **equals or greater than**.

5. Click on the following ellipses (...) and enter 100. Hit your *Enter* key.
6. Then, change **ALL** to **ANY** in the condition description.
7. Click on the green + icon nested within this condition.
8. Select **Category** from the drop-down menu.
9. Click on **is** and select **is one of** from the drop-down menu.
10. Click on the following ellipses (...) and either using the list icon or by typing the category IDs of the categories you wish to use, select the **Tops** category and the all subcategories within.

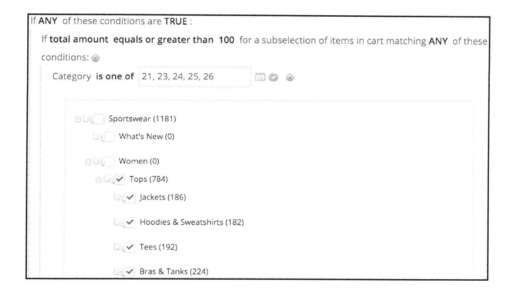

 It's a good idea to select all the subcategories as well because you may have items that are only assigned to a subcategory and not to the top-level category.

11. Once you select your categories, click on the green checkmark icon to save your choices.

    Next, we need to add the "or" condition that tests whether the customer has three or more women's apparel items in their cart.

12. Click on the leftmost green + icon.
13. Select **Products subselection** in the resulting drop-down menu.

14. Select **equals or greater than** for the comparison value.
15. Enter 3 for the amount.
16. Change **ALL to ANY** in the condition description.
17. Then, click the nested green + icon.
18. Select **Category** from the drop-down menu.
19. Click on **is** and select **is one of** from the drop-down choices.
20. Click on the ellipses (...) and select all the categories within the women's apparel section.

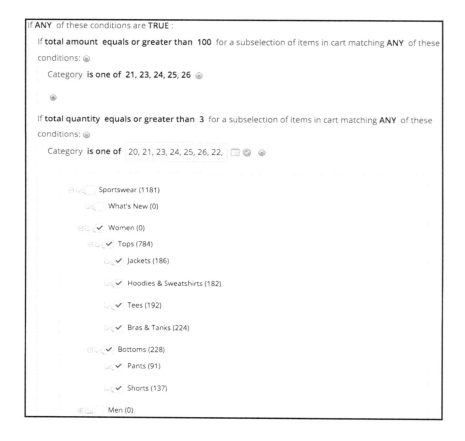

21. Click on **Save and Continue Edit** to save your work up to this point.

Once your conditions are set, your Conditions panel should look similar to the following image:

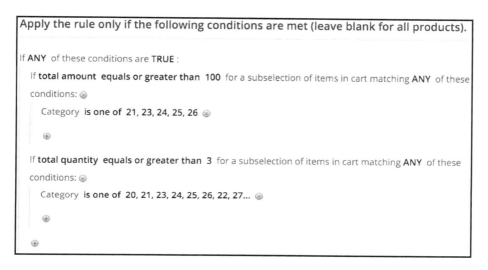

Now, we can move on to specifying the actions that will take place for the shopping carts that match our conditions.

Defining the rule's actions

There are two parts to a rule's actions:

1. The amount discounted
2. The products for which the discount is to be applied

This is important to understand as many are confused by the fact that action conditions appear to be very similar to the rule conditions we created before. The conditions in this panel dictate which products qualify for the discounts.

In other words, as in our case, we will use one set of conditions to qualify the shopping cart and another set within the **Actions** panel to identify which products the discount will be applied for. These conditions are different. If they were the same—for example, if you're discounting a shopping cart containing $100 or more in products—then you do not have to add any conditions to the **Actions** panel.

Let's now configure our **Actions** panel for our needs:

1. For **Apply**, select the default, **Percent of product price discount**.

   Let's go over the various choices here so that you have an idea as to which discount will work best with your purposes. Any value that is required will be entered into the **Discount Amount** field.

   - **Percent of product price discount**: This subtracts a percentage of discount from the price of the applicable products
   - **Fixed amount discount**: This subtracts a fixed amount from the price of the products
   - **Fixed amount discount for whole cart**: The fixed amount entered here will be discounted from the entire cart total (you can specify whether the discount applies to shipping elsewhere on this panel)
   - **Buy X Get Y Free (discount amount is Y)**: You can specify that if a customer buys X quantity of a product (entered into the **Discount Qty Step (Buy X)** field), they will receive Y quantity of the same product for free

2. Enter 20 into the **Discount Amount** field. You do not need to enter "%" for percentage discounts.
3. As we are not limiting the number of the same item for which the discount may be applied, we will set **Maximum Qty Discount is Applied To** to 0.
4. The **Discount Qty Step (Buy X)** option does not apply for our case (refer to the preceding section regarding the Buy X Get Y Free discount choice).
5. Leave **Apply to Shipping Amount** as **No**.
6. Set **Discard subsequent rules** to **Yes**. We do not want other offers to apply if this discount is used.

 If the priority of your rule is lower than another rule, the higher priority rule will still be applied. This setting only applies to lower priority rules.

7. Set **Free Shipping** to **For shipment with matching items** as our example discount also gives the customer free shipping for the entire qualifying order.

For free shipping to work, you have to have at least one **Free Shipping** method configured. Refer to `Chapter 4`, *Preparing to Sell* for more information on shipping.

8. Click on **Save and Continue Edit** to save your settings so far.

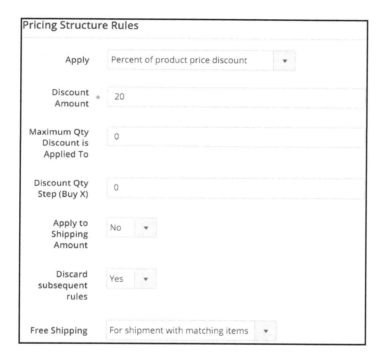

The next part of our **Actions** configuration is to designate which products the discount will be applied to. In our case, any women's apparel (up to the three we set in the upper part of the panel).

Using the same methodology we use in the **Conditions** panel, our **Actions** panel rules, when completed, will look similar to the following:

Apply the rule only to cart items matching the following conditions (leave blank for all items).

If **ANY** of these conditions are **TRUE** :

  Category is one of 20, 21, 23, 24, 25, 26, 22, 27... ⊗

  ⊕

Modifying the rule's labels

While you could use the name of the rule as what displays to customers, it's probably more prudent to compose a discount label that more succinctly describes the discount. Furthermore, as in our example, we need different labels for each of the foreign language sites on which we will sell sportswear.

For our example, we will label our discount for our customers as `Save 20% & Free Shipping!` Perform the following steps:

1. In the **Labels** panel, enter `Save 20% & Free Shipping!` in **Default Rule Label for All Store Views**.
2. As we can use the same label for our English Store View, we can leave **Sportswear English View** blank.
3. For **Sportswear French View**, we might enter (and, again, our French and German are not polished at all!) `Économisez 20% et livraison gratuite!`.
4. In **Sportswear German View**, we might use `Sie sparen 20% & Kostenloser Versand!`.

Then, of course, we will click on **Save and Continue Edit**. Our **Labels** panel now looks similar to the following screenshot:

Generating coupon codes

In our example, we want to create 100 unique coupon codes that we can send to our selected customers. Magento does an amazing job of helping you generate codes and also keeps track of how many times the codes are used.

To begin, go to the **Manage Coupon Codes** panel. Let's assume we want to create codes that are alphanumeric (both letters and numbers), 12 characters long, and have a prefix of ASW and a suffix of F20. Our coupon pattern would be ASW-XXX-XXX-F20, where "XXX" is a unique alphanumeric code. To configure this, we will set up the parameters for the codes and then click on **Generate** to allow Magento to create the 100 unique codes we need. Perform the following steps:

1. In **Coupon Qty**, enter 100.

> For testing purposes, and particularly if these are single, use coupon codes, you should generate a few more than you need. In this case, we might want to generate 110 or 120 codes just so that we can thoroughly test the code. Take a look at the next section about testing.

2. Our **Code Length** value is 6 (we do not count the hyphens or the prefix and suffix as we will specify these a bit later).
3. For **Code Format**, select **Alphanumeric**.

4. In **Code Prefix**, enter ASW- (we will use this for Acme Sportswear).

5. In Code Suffix, enter -F20 (for Free & 20% off).

The use of a prefix and/or suffix is purely optional. If you're using unique coupon codes, you may want to use some designators that will help you identify whether the code is a valid code for the order. When an order is viewed in your backend, it will show what codes, if any, were applied to the order. If you only use randomly generated codes without other designators, you might not be able to easily determine which actual discount rule was applied. If you want hyphens before or after a prefix/suffix, you need to include it in the appropriate fields.

6. As we want a hyphen inserted into our codes, we can enter 3 in **Dash Every X Characters**.

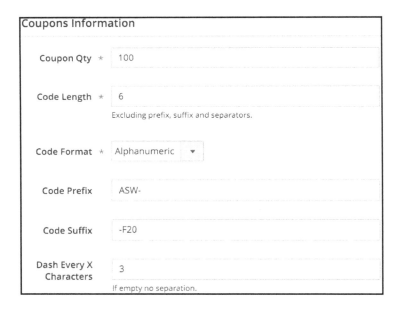

Now we can click on **Generate** to create our 100 unique codes. Once generated, you should see 100 records created in the lower portion of the panel. Although your codes will be different (they are randomly generated, after all), your list should look similar to ours.

Customers may enter codes using either the lower or upper case. The code *asw-xqu-u7i-f20* will work just as well as *ASW-XQU-U7I-F20* or *AsW-xQu-U7I-f20*.

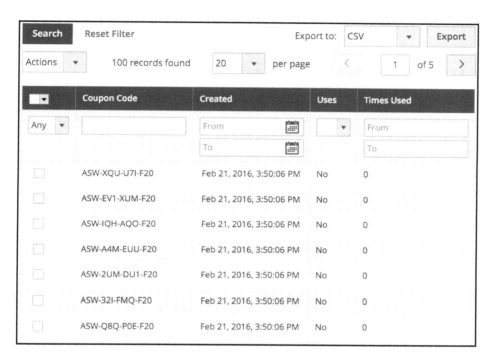

Using the export tool at the top of your list, you can now export our codes and use them with your e-mail program to send these codes to your customers.

 Unfortunately, Magento 2 does not have a native means of sending your unique codes to your customers. You will have to use third-party e-mail solutions or extensions if you wish to send these codes to your customers.

Testing the rule

As with any configuration you make in Magento, you should test and retest to make sure your settings are correct. Try various tests, too. In developeres, these are called *use cases*.

If your coupon code is only valid at a future date, you should change the start date to *TODAY* and then change to the future date once you complete the testing.

The more you test, the more confident you'll feel that your rule is valid.

Newsletter subscriptions

Once a new customer is acquired, it makes great sense to keep them interested in your offerings so that they will return again to make a purchase from your online store. The *cost of acquisition* for a sale is far less with a repeat transaction.

Magento 2 can help you keep your brand in the forefront of your customers' minds with basic e-mail newsletter tools. With these tools, you can:

- Allow customers to subscribe
- Create newsletter templates
- Schedule the sending of your newsletter
- Manage your subscribers

Magento will be the first to admit that their newsletter tools are pretty basic. If you want to be more sophisticated in how you construct your newsletters, segment your customers, and more, you should consider a more robust third-party tool. We use MailChimp (`http://www.mailchimp.com`), a leading e-mail system that makes it easy to manage campaigns. It's fun to use as well.

To connect your Magento 2 store to MailChimp, we recommend the MageMonkey for Magento 2 extension (`http://store.ebizmarts.com/magemonkey-magento2.html`). Ebizmarts, the creator of this extension, worked closely with MailChimp. The extension also adds e-mails for abandoned carts, supports multiple MailChimp lists, and creates autoresponders-e-mails for customer birthdays, related products, and product reviews. Also, best of all, at the time of writing, the extension was offered for free!

Subscribing customers

In `Chapter 2`, *Settings and Configurations,* we covered the newsletter settings in the **Stores** | **Configuration** | **Customers** | **Newsletter** panel. The newsletter function is enabled by default in Magento 2. As long as you have a newsletter subscription form on your site, your customers can subscribe and be added to your newsletter list.

By default, a subscription form is placed in the footer of the base theme. If you use a third-party theme, the subscription form may be placed in another location.

Ask your Magento developer for assistance if you wish to relocate or disable the newsletter subscription form. It may require the modification of the theme files on your server.

Creating newsletter templates

Before you can send a newsletter, you have to create a newsletter template. This template contains your marketing message but can also contain dynamic content.

To begin, go to **Marketing** | **Newsletter Templates** in your Magento backend. Click on **Add New Template**. On the **Template Information** panel, you will see the following fields:

- **Template Name**: Enter a name for the newsletter that is meaningful to you, as shown in your list of templates. You might use something similar to `Marketing Newsletter, Feb 2016` or `Spring Sale Announcement, 2016`.
- **Template Subject**: This is the subject that will appear in the e-mail subject received by your customers. Use something that is enticing without sounding *spammy*.
- **Sender Name**: The From e-mail shown in the e-mail header will contain a name and an e-mail address, sometimes in the form `Acme Support <support@acmefurniture.com>`. This field is the *name* part (for example, Acme Support).
- **Sender Email**: This is the e-mail address part of the From address. It is also the e-mail address to which the replies to your newsletter will be sent.

Some people use *noreply@* as a sending e-mail address. Some spam filters will object to this, and if you're intent on customer service, this is considered poor form.

- **Template Content**: As with other complex text fields in Magento, this one has a WYSIWYG editor to give you several tools for building an attractive and meaningful e-mail newsletter. As with the blocks and CMS pages we discussed in Chapter 7, *Content and SEO*, you can insert variables and widgets as well. This gives you the ability to insert products, category links, and more!

When creating a new template, you'll see the default content for inserting a variable for an unsubscribe link. This is key if you want to avoid violating antispam standards. However, there are more guidelines you should follow if you want your newsletters to be considered as valid e-mails by your subscribed customers. A good resource for compliance guidance can be found at http://kb.mailchimp.com/accounts#Compl iance_Tips.

- **Template Styles**: If you wish to add CSS styles to your newsletter content, you can add the CSS styling in this field.

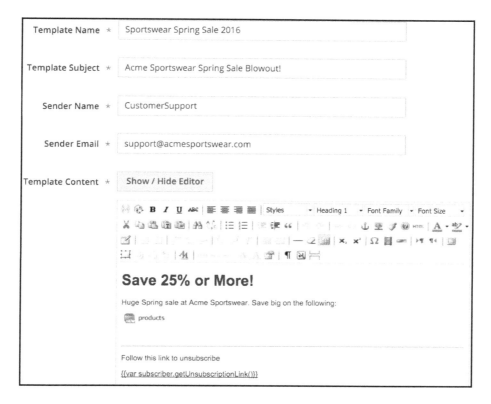

Once you complete your template, you can click on **Preview Template** to view your newsletter as it will appear to your customers.

Scheduling your newsletter

When you're ready to schedule your newsletter to send, go to **Marketing | Newsletter Templates**. In the **Action** column to the right of the newsletter you wish to send, select **Queue Newsletter** in the drop-down menu. The screen will redirect you to the **Queue Information** panel.

Here, you can select the date on which you wish to send your newsletter, select the Store Views for whose subscribers you wish to receive your newsletter, and review the contents of your newsletter.

Once you make your selection, click on **Save Newsletter** to add it to the internal queue. Magento will send your newsletters to your chosen subscribers on the date you selected.

To view your newsletter queue and the status of your queued newsletters, go to **Marketing | Newsletter Queue**.

 At the time of this writing, there is no means of cancelling a queued newsletter. You can, however, set **Queue Date Start** to blank, which will prevent it from being sent.

Checking for problems

Once your newsletter is sent, you can take a look at how well it is sent and check for any problems by going to **Reports | Newsletter Problems Report**. If any problems are found, a report identifying each error will appear in this list.

Managing your subscribers

Under **Marketing** | **Newsletter Subscribers**, you can view all or a filtered subset of your newsletter subscribers. This can be helpful if you wish to see how many have come from the various Stores in your installation. You can also unsubscribe customers from this screen.

As with most other *grid* listings in Magento, you can export your subscriber list to use for other purposes.

Transactional e-mails

As customers make purchases in your store, Magento sends, based on your configurations, a number of e-mails to notify customers about their purchases. There are also e-mails to recover passwords, create accounts, and more.

Magento installs basic templates for all these **transactional e-mails**. You can create new e-mail templates to use for your stores that reflect your branding and messaging. In Magento 2, this is quite easy to do.

 Many new Magento store owners will simply use the default e-mails that are installed with Magento. While these e-mails are not bad, you should invest the time to modify each to meet your specific brand and design.

When you first go to **Marketing** | **Email Templates**, you'll see an empty list. This is normal. The base templates installed with Magento will not appear in this list, but they are there, nonetheless. E-mail templates can also be included in Magento themes added to your installation. These will also not be shown in the list but will be available for customization.

The process of customizing e-mail templates is as follows:

1. Create a new template.
2. Apply an existing template to your new template.
3. Modify it to accommodate your needs.

Once you create your new e-mail template, you can assign it for use as sales e-mails, customer account e-mails, and so on.

You can create new e-mail templates for the following purposes:

- **Payment Failed***
- **Contact Us Form**

- Forgot Password
- New Account
- New Account Confirmation Key
- New Account Confirmed
- New Account Without Password
- Remind Password
- Reset Password
- Currency Update Warning*
- Subscription Confirmation
- Subscription Success
- Unsubscription Success
- Cron Error Warning*
- Price Alert
- Stock Alert
- Credit Memo Update
- Credit Memo Update for Guest (purchaser who does not log in)
- Invoice Update
- Invoice Update for Guest
- New Credit Memo
- New Credit Memo for Guest
- New Invoice
- New Invoice for Guest
- New Order
- New Order for Guest
- Order Update
- Order Update for Guest
- Shipment Update
- Shipment Update for Guest
- Send Product Link to Friend
- Sitemap Generation Warnings*
- Forgot Admin Password
- Reset Password
- Wish List Sharing

As you can note, Magento has quite a number of e-mails. The items in this list with an asterisk (*) are e-mails that are not sent to your customers but rather sent to you or someone you designate. These e-mails are to alert your team when something doesn't go quite right.

There are also two additional templates that are used to create the headers and footers for your e-mails. In other words, you can manage the top and bottom of your e-mails without having to modify every single e-mail if, for example, you want to change your logo or phone number.

To illustrate how to do this, let's create a new e-mail template for our Sportswear store. We will begin by modifying the header and footer for our Sportswear store and then creating a new New Order e-mail template.

Creating a new header template

On the **Email Templates** panel, click on **Add New Template**. At the top of the **New Template** panel, you'll notice an area titled **Load default template**. Here, you can select the base template, or a template provided by a theme, and load it into the **New Template** panel for modification.

You could, of course, create a template from scratch, but it can be a real time saver to modify an existing template.

For our new header, select **Header** and click on **Load Template**. This will load the base header template into our New Template form.

Currently Used For	Stores -> Configuration -> Design -> Emails -> Header Template (Default Config)
Template Name *	
Template Subject *	Header
Template Content *	`<!DOCTYPE html PUBLIC "-//W3C//DTD XHTML 1.0 Strict//EN" "http://www.w3.org/TR/xhtml1/DTD/xhtml1-strict.dtd"> <html xmlns="http://www.w3.org/1999/xhtml"> <head> <meta http-equiv="Content-Type" content="text/html; charset=utf-8" /> <meta name="viewport" content="initial-scale=1.0, width=device-width" /> <meta http-equiv="X-UA-Compatible" content="IE=edge" /> <style type="text/css"> {{var template_styles	raw}} {{css file="css/email.css"}} </style> </head> <body> {{inlinecss file="css/email-inline.css"}} <!-- Begin wrapper table -->`
Template Styles	

Let's first review the fields shown on this screen:

- **Currently Used For**: Not actually an editable field, this shows where this e-mail is assigned for use. In this case, we can note that the header template we loaded is used in the configuration at **Stores** | **Configuration** | **Design** | **Emails** | **Header Template** at the *Default* configuration scope. This means that the header template is used as the default header for all e-mails in your installation. Once we build our Sportswear header (and footer) templates, we will assign them at the Sportswear website configuration scope so that they will be used for all Sportswear e-mails.
- **Template Name**: Use a name that is useful when shown in the list of e-mail templates. In our example here, we might use `Header (Sportswear)`.

- **Template Subject**: For e-mails, this is the subject that will appear in the e-mail sent. For the header and footer, leave this as shown so that they are properly included in generated e-mails.
- **Template Content**: It is into this field that you will make any changes to layout and content.

 As you can note, there is no WYSIWYG editor in this panel. If you are not well-versed in HTML, you should have your Magento developer assist you in editing your e-mail templates.

Once we modify the header to our liking, we can save it by clicking on **Save Template**. If we look at our list of **Email Templates**, we will now have the one template listed.

ID	Template	Added	Updated	Subject	Template Type	Action
		From	From		▼	
		To	To			
1	Header (Sportswear)	Feb 28, 2016, 3:41:53 PM	Feb 28, 2016, 3:41:53 PM	Header	HTML	Preview

Assigning the e-mail header and footer

If we click on the template and view its detail, we will be able to see that it has no **Currently Used For** field as it is not assigned to any particular Website or Store entity. Once we create our Sportswear footer (it is not necessarily required to create both to be able to create and assign only header or footer), we can now assign these to our Sportswear Website entity so that they appear for each Store View. Perform the following steps:

 This capability gives you the ability to create multiple language e-mails as well as to translate your website for your international customers.

1. Go to **Stores** | **Configuration** | **General** | **Design** in your backend.
2. Change your **Store View** setting to **Sportswear Website**.

1. Then, expand the **Emails** panel.
2. Beside **Header Template** and **Footer Template**, unselect the **Use Default** checkbox.
3. For **Header Template**, select **Header (Sportswear)** in the drop-down menu.
4. For **Footer Template**, select **Footer (Sportswear)**.
5. Click on **Save Config**.

We have now assigned our new e-mail header and footer to all outgoing e-mails related to the Sportswear stores. If you view the detail for your header and footer e-mail templates, they will now display a **Currently Used For** value.

Currently Used For	Stores -> Configuration -> Design -> Emails -> Header Template (Sportswear Website)

Creating a new e-mail template

Now that we have created our special header and footer, we can create our New Order e-mail for our Sportswear customers. Perform the following steps:

1. Return to **Marketing** | **Email Templates**.
2. Click on **Add New Template**.
3. Load the **New Order** default template. Note that for the Magento Luma theme, there is an installed *New Order* template specific to the Luma theme. As we're using the Luma theme for our example stores, we will choose **New Order (Magento/luma)** as our default template.
4. Give your new e-mail template a suitable name. In our case, we'll use `New Order (Sportswear)`.
5. For our **Template Subject**, we will adjust it a bit by replacing its default contents with `Thanks for Your {{var store.getFrontendName()}} Order!`.

As you can note, the subject contains a Magento variable that will dynamically include the name of the Store. As we will name our Sportswear Stores as Sportswear English View, Sportswear French View, and Sportswear German View, we may not want to use the dynamic Store View name as these don't sound particularly consumer-friendly. For our example, we would prefer to use `Thanks for Your Acmes Sportswear Order!`

6. Make any other changes you wish to make to the **Template Content** and **Template Styles**.
7. Click on **Save Template**.

As with the header and footer, we will now assign this e-mail to the appropriate sales e-mail.

8. Go to **Stores** | **Configuration** | **Sales** | **Sales Emails**.
9. Then, change **Store View** to **Sportswear Website**.
10. Open the **Order** panel.
11. For **New Order Confirmation Template**, unselect **Use Default** and select **New Order (Sportswear)** in the drop-down menu.
12. Click on **Save** Config.

We have now created a modified New Order template for our logged-in purchasers and assigned it to our Sportswear Store entities.

There are different e-mails for logged-in and guest customers because logged-in customer e-mails can include links to the customer's account. Guest customers cannot log in to your Magento store as no account is set up when a customers checks out as a guest.

Summary

Magento provides you, the store owner, with powerful tools to promote products, offer discounts and reward certain customers, power that may seem complicated but, with a bit of practice, can help stimulate sales.

Your communication with customers is very important as any contact with a purchaser is a reflection of your brand. It's not a hyperbole to say your reputation demands as much on how well you *speak* with your audience as it does on the products you sell.

In this chapter, we explored:

- Creating promotional discounts and pricing rules
- Managing newsletters and subscribers
- Modifying outgoing e-mails.

With these skills well in hand, you can significantly impact the success of your store.

In our next chapter, we will discuss ways to add security to your store as well as administrative tasks that will improve your store's performance.

9
Security and Administration

As the proprietor of an online store, you are ultimately responsible for its success. A part of this responsibility is to make sure your store is both secure and operating at peak performance. Just as you're the one who would lock up a brick-and-mortar store at the end of the day, it's important that you safeguard your online store from cyber thieves as well as those who will access your Magento 2 backend.

It's also important to optimize your store for speed to give your online customers the very best shopping experience possible. No one likes having to unduly wait for pages to load.

In this chapter, we will go over the configurations that you can handle yourself:

- Using **SSL encryption**
- Securing your server
- Configuring user permissions
- Magento indexing
- Optimization settings

We should mention that your developer should be involved in these configurations as some may require server adjustments or file changes.

 We can't overemphasize the value a great Magento developer can add to the success of your store. While there are lots of developers who claim Magento expertise, don't be afraid to ask for references and confirm their Magento 2 certifications at `https://www.magentocommerce.com/certi fication/directory`. It takes a lot more than PHP and MySQL skills to be successful at developing Magento stores.

Let's start now by discussing SSL encryption and how it adds value to your Magento store.

Using SSL encryption

If you've used the Web for any amount of time, you must have heard a lot about online security. In fact, shopping online (or banking, healthcare, and more) would not exist if there wasn't a way of securing information sent over the Internet.

Without getting into a deep lesson on how security works, we do want to give you a primer on the various terms and concepts that will help you understand how security works with your Magento store.

When your customers come to your store and wish to submit confidential information, such as in credit card payment, your server needs to allow this information to be sent from your customer's computer to your server (and on to the payment processor in this case) in a manner that will prevent anyone outside of your system from intercepting and reading this information.

On the web, the most common and convenient method is through SSL encryption. **Secure Socket Layer** (**SSL**) means that any information sent between two points on the Internet—such as your customer and your Magento store—is encrypted using very complex algorithms. The information is *unencrypted* on each end using certain keys that can only be used by each end of the connection.

When you visit a web page that is SSL encrypted, you usually see a small lock icon in the address bar of your browser to indicate that any information retrieved or sent is encrypted at the origin and unencrypted when received.

The SSL certificate

Encryption is created on your server by installing an **SSL certificate**. This certificate actually contains several special, encoded files that provide the customer's browser with encryption keys and proof that your certificate is valid and backed by one of several **root certificates**. Root certificates validate that your secured site domain is proven to belong to you and that the encryption used is truly secure.

Think of the root certificate provider as a country's central bank. The central bank guarantees that the money we use, the bills and coins, are legal tender and backed by the government to be valid for trade.

When you obtain an SSL certificate, the entity that grants the certificate, likewise, gives your customers the confidence that their information is encrypted and secure, at least as far as transmission over the Internet is concerned.

> Later in this chapter, we will give you guidance on how to check on the security of your Magento server.

Obtaining an SSL certificate

Your developer or hosting provider may have resources to help you obtain your SSL certificate. You can also check with the company with whom you registered your domain (for example, GoDaddy or Google Domains).

> We recently transferred all our domains (and we own dozens) to Google Domains (`https://domains.google.com`). While not the least expensive, we trust Google's ability to avoid downtime, and their domain management tools are much easier to use. Furthermore, we're not inundated with tons of ads and offers. If you have a Google app or Gmail account, you can easily register or transfer domains to Google Domains. Google doesn't provide SSL certificates yet, though.
> Another company we use that provides low-cost SSL certificates is DNSimple (`https://dnsimple.com`). This is very easy to use, and their support is good too. If you prefer a non-Google solution and appreciate responsive support, you might like DNSimple.

To obtain an SSL certificate, you need to make sure you are the registered owner of your domain and that the e-mail address associated with your domain is one you can access. The SSL certificate provider will send a confirmation of your request to the e-mail address listed on your domain.

You can check the information listed with your domain by going to `https://domains.google.com` and entering your domain on the home page. Only enter the primary domain without www. As you already own the domain, the results page will show that the domain is *not* available. Click on the small three dot menu to the far right of your domain name and select **Look up WHOIS**.

On the WHOIS page, you should see the registrant information for your domain. If this information is not correct, you should correct it with your domain registrar before applying for an SSL certificate.

 If you added privacy protection to your domain, your personal and company information will not show up on WHOIS. You may need to turn off privacy on your domain in order to obtain an SSL certificate as the certificate provider has to validate that you are who you say you are when applying for an SSL certificate.

You can get a certificate from many providers, and it is important that you obtain one of sufficient strength for today's e-commerce. SSL certificates should use the latest encryption standards, or your customers may receive browser warnings.

Additionally, SSL certificates come in many flavors:

- **Domain validated**: These are quick and easy to obtain. The provider simply confirms that you own the domain. These are usually sufficient for e-commerce in 99% of the cases.
- **Company validated**: These are a bit more expensive as the provider will request documentation about your company. These provide a bit more confidence for shoppers, but unless shoppers actually look up your certificate, they won't see a difference between this and the domain validated certificate in terms of their interaction with your store.
- **Extended validation**: These certificates are usually quite pricey. The provider conducts much more extensive validation of your company. If you use these certificates, online customers will see a green lock icon in the browser address bar.
- **Wildcard certificates**: If you want to secure more than your domain (and the www version of your domain), you may want to get a wildcard certificate. This certificate would allow you to use multiple **subdomains** on the same server, such as `help.domain.com`, `downloads.domain.com`, and so on. You cannot use a wildcard for multiple primary domains, such as `domain1.com`, `domain2.com`, and so on.

- **Multidomain certificates**: If you need to use multiple primary domains on the same server, you can opt for this type. However, some older browsers may not accept a multidomain certificate, although we find this to be a very, very small set.

Now that you have a better understanding of SSL encryption and certificates, we suggest that you consult with your Magento developer or hosting provider on the best course of action for your particular business needs. It's critical that you get the proper type of certificate for your server and that it provides the appropriate level of security.

Securing your server

Your Magento developer should be skilled enough to have installed Magento 2 on your server in such a manner that all known vulnerabilities are eliminated.

 Magento, Inc. is generally good at attacking any discovered vulnerabilities in their platform by issuing patches and guidance to the user community. No server is 100% secure as some vulnerabilities may not have yet been discovered. However, you and your developer can make sure you address all the known possibilities.

However, any breach of security ultimately rests with you, the store owner. You should ask your developer for confirmation of the following:

- **File permissions**: Are the files on your server properly configured to prevent outside access? (Hackers love to find unprotected files.)
- **Database access:** Is any outside access to your database limited by the IP number?
- **Developer access**: If your developer is employing other developers, what controls are put in place to control access? Is this access eliminated once the development work is completed?
- **Versioning**: Your developer should not be working directly on your live server. Instead, development work should be done using a versioning systems, such as git or svn. In this manner, any code updates to your server would have to match what is in the code repository, thereby thwarting any unauthorized code modifications.
- **SSH access**: Your developer may use SSH to access your server for configuration purposes. This access should be particular to a user and limited by IP.

One final note: never give your master credentials to your developer unless you completely trust their expertise and confidentiality. It's better to create individual access accounts for anyone outside of your company and in direct control. Your hosting provider can help you set these up or show you how to manage additional server users.

We had a situation once where we hired a developer through an online freelance site to assist us with a client installation. As usual, we set up individual access accounts for this developer. In a short time, we discovered that the developer was billing us for work they did not do, and we severed the relationship. At the same time, when we were eliminating their access accounts, we received an e-mail from this unscrupulous person threatening to compromise our client's site if we contested their invoice. As we were able to lock them out, we feared nothing, and nothing happened to damage our client's site. The developer was blocked from using the freelance service, and the service even refunded all the money we had paid. The lesson here: never give an outside person the "keys to the kingdom" unless you fully trust their abilities, ethics, and reputation. Also, always have a contract or terms that further protect you.

Configuring user permissions

As with developers, you may want to limit your exposure to damage by giving users of your Magento 2 backend limited access to only the tools and capabilities they need. We know it's easier to simply share your login credentials with your staff, but if or when there comes a time to dismiss a staff person—or if they leave for another job opportunity—you must change your login credentials if you want to eliminate their access.

Additionally, sharing credentials reduces accountability in terms of knowing who did what and when.

The community version of Magento 2 provides you with the tools to provide credentials to as many users as you need as well as create roles that limit access to the features and functions of your store's backend.

Managing roles

In Magento, each user is assigned a *role*. A role defines the access that a user has to various parts of the backend as well as their capability to change or delete certain records. When your store is initially created, an **Administrator role** is created, and your initial owner account is assigned this role. The Administrator role gives you full access to everything in the backend of your store.

 Never share your Administrator credentials with anyone! If your developer created your store, change the password as soon as you log in. We'll discuss creating a Developer role a bit later in this section.

Roles are listed under **System | User Roles** in your Magento 2 backend.

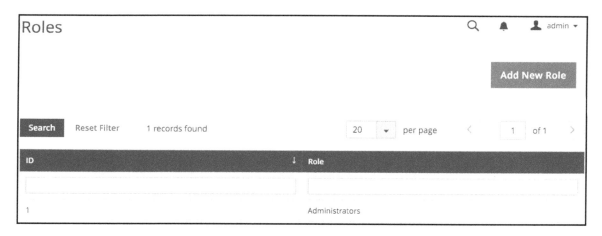

Let's create a new example role for a staff person who will manage orders. We want to give them the capability to manage orders and customers, but they don't need the ability to change any product or other store information. Perform the following steps:

1. In the User Roles panel, click on **Add New Role**.
2. For **Role Name**, enter `Order Manager`.

3. Click on **Role Resources** in the sidebar menu to the left. For our purposes in this example, we'll leave **Resource Access** set to **Custom**.

4. You can, of course, click on any you prefer, but we will select the ones shown in the following image as we want our order manager to access all the parts relating to sales. (For brevity, we collapsed the sections that we will not select):

5. Then, click on **Save Role**.

If you give some thought to your team and functions, you can probably construct several roles for your organization. For instance, if you have someone who simply needs to view orders but not manage them, you could create an "Order Analyst" role and unselect all the items that create, edit, or cancel orders and customers. In this way, you can prevent accidental record changes.

Do not skip the process of creating roles. We've seen too many store owners that simply give others full access of their backend and then face severe problems when someone without proper training does it wrong.

Creating a developer role

If your developer needs access to your backend, we suggest you avoid assigning the Administrators role to their user account (and, especially, don't give them your own login credentials!).

Rather, you can create a Developers role and assign them all capabilities *except* those that perform the following:

- **Create, edit, or cancel orders on a live store**: This functionality should be fully tested on a development or staging server. You don't want developers accidentally affecting your cash flow!
- **Manage permissions**: You should be the only one who can create or edit users on your system.
- **Manage the Encryption key**: This is the "key" to the sensitive information on your system. Changing this could have severe ramifications.

For any role, think of it this way: if you cannot immediately delete a user from your system, how much damage could they do if they wanted? We realize that this is something you'd rather not consider, but for your live store, you should.

Creating users

With your roles created, you can now create the actual user accounts that will allow your team to log into your store's backend. To view your users, go to **System** | **All Users**.

As you can see, when this store was initially installed, the developer created a default owner account.

We strongly recommend that you use a nonstandard username for your Administrator account. If this sample store were a live site, we would immediately change this account's username to something less obvious—perhaps something similar to acme_admin or acmeowner. Using a nonstandard username can help thwart hacker attempts to access your store backend.

To create a new user, perform the following steps:

1. Click on **Add New User**.
2. Fill in all the required fields shown.

Don't be afraid to use a strong password for your users. You don't want outsiders to gain access to your store by guessing a common password.

3. Enter your password in the **Your Password** field at the bottom.

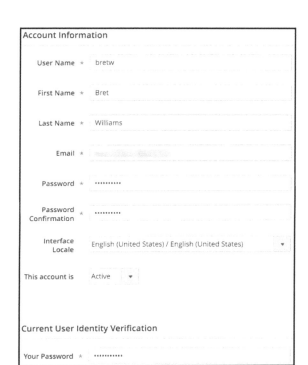

2. Click on **User Role** in the sidebar menu to the left.
3. Next, select the role you wish to assign to your user. Users can only be assigned to one single role.
4. Click on **Save User**.

Your user will not be sent an e-mail when the account is created. You need to communicate the username and password to your user separately.

User security

Magento 2 has improved security features over Magento 1.x. If you go to **Stores** | **Configuration** | **Advanced** | **Admin** and expand the **Security** panel, you'll see the security settings you can control. This panel was also discussed in Chapter 2, *Settings and Configurations*.

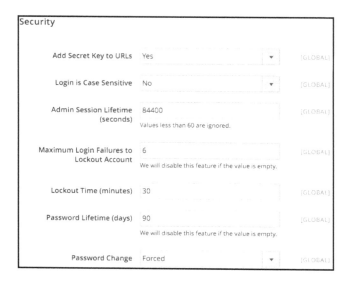

As you can see, you can help prevent hacking attempts by locking users out of the backend if they fail to log in correctly. If a user gets locked out, you can "release" the lock by going to **System | Locked Users**.

 If a user is locked out and the individual says they weren't trying to log in, then a hacker is attempting to guess the user's password. You should change the username for your user and review the strength of their password. Usernames, as well as passwords, should never be shared.

Magento indexing

Magento has a very complex data architecture. Data is broken down into hundreds of data tables as part of its intent to provide true flexibility and customization. A single product record, for example, may be stored across dozens of tables, each having a distinct purpose of storing a particular aspect of the data that, when combined, comprises the final product to display to your customers.

If Magento had to look up data across all these tables every time someone visited a product detail page, the rendering of the page would be very slow. As your site traffic increases, the slowing down becomes more and more noticeable.

Therefore, in order to provide fewer lookups for each rendered page, Magento indexes the data by combining the data from all the various related tables into only a few tables. This greatly increases the speed of your store.

In Magento 2, this indexing can occur whenever you change a record in your store or automatically according to a timed schedule, which is called a **cron job**. The process of configuring your server's cron job is beyond the scope of this book. However, it's important that you have your developer review and test your store's indexing functionality. Without proper indexing, you will penalize your customers or your data will not be properly up to date.

You can view the latest status of your indexing by going to **System** | **Index Management**.

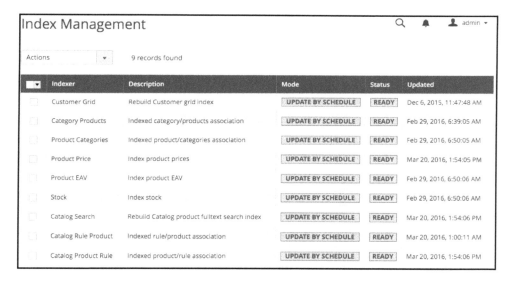

Magento 2's indexing is more intelligent now, too. It only reindexes the information that needs reindexing. This helps reduce the load on your server.

Optimizing your store

To compete for consumer attention, your site needs to render quickly. Today's customers are not patient. They expect sites to "pop" onto their screens. They're eager to shop, but they don't want to slog through a site waiting for pages to render.

There are several things that can affect site speed, and they are as follows:

- **The hosting environment**: The setup of your web server is critically important. Be sure that you work with one that understands how to configure a server for Magento as the platform is demanding of resources. Cheap, shared hosting accounts usually don't work at all for Magento.

 For most Magento stores, MageMojo (`https://magemojo.com`) is our preferred hosting provider. They only focus on hosting Magento stores. We use them as our sole provider because, in large part, of their excellent service.

- **The theme code**: Some themes, while pretty, are "heavy" in terms of how the code is constructed. Many include JavaScript libraries for fancy features even on pages that don't use the feature. Others add extensions for various features that can weigh down your installation. It's often better to find a lean, flexible theme that you can design to your needs rather than trying to find one built for a specific vertical (for instance, jewelry or apparel). You should first try using the theme included with Magento 2 and check whether it can meet your needs.

 At the time of writing, there aren't many new Magento 2 themes available. We're waiting anxiously for a Magento 2 version of the Ultimo theme (`http://goo.gl/mj6lR8`). It is by far our favorite for Magento 1.x, and the developers informed us that they are working on a Magento 2 version. Hopefully, it will be released soon!

- **Extensions**: Whenever you want to add a new extension to your store, have your developer install and test it on a development installation. Many a time, extensions can affect site speed, security, or reliability. Don't rush to install on a live server until you do your due diligence.
- **Images**: Related to your theme, the images you use—particularly for nonproduct images—need to be optimized for size and compression. Placing a 2000-px-wide image on a CMS page where you set it to show at 300-px width means that your customers will have to wait for a very large image to download before it can be displayed. It would be better to resize your image to a 300-px width before placing it on the page.
- **Configurations**: As we'll cover next, you and your developer should review all backend configurations to make sure they are set for maximum optimization.

If your developer truly knows Magento, they can certainly optimize your store installation for speed. We covered many of the configuration panels in Chapter 2, *Settings and Configurations*. However, let's go over a list of specific items that you should review:

- **Indexing**: As we discussed previously, indexing is critical to performance.
- **Caching**: Magento uses caching to deliver pages to customers without having to regenerate the entire page each time. Caching is also a consideration when choosing a hosting provider.
- **HTML minification**: Magento can reduce the size of the pages sent to customers' browsers by eliminating extra white space and lines. Compare the two code sections in the following figures; the first image is the HTML code for our home page without minification, and the second shows the same code minified by Magento. The increase in speed with minification is nominal, but every little bit helps!

```
<div class="block block-search">
    <div class="block block-title"><strong>Search</strong></div>
    <div class="block block-content">
        <form class="form minisearch" id="search_mini_form"
action="http://m2.novusweb.com/catalogsearch/result/" method="get">
            <div class="field search">
                <label class="label" for="search" data-role="minisearch-label">
                    <span>Search</span>
                </label>
                <div class="control">
                    <input id="search"
                            data-mage-init='{"quickSearch":{
                                "formSelector":"#search_mini_form",
                                "url":"http://m2.novusweb.com/search/ajax/suggest/",
                                "destinationSelector":"#search_autocomplete"}
                            }'
                            type="text"
                            name="q"
                            value=""
                            placeholder="Search entire store here..."
                            class="input-text"
                            maxlength="128"
                            role="combobox"
                            aria-haspopup="false"
                            aria-autocomplete="both"
                            autocomplete="off"/>
                    <div id="search_autocomplete" class="search-autocomplete"></div>
                    <div class="nested">
    <a class="action advanced" href="http://m2.novusweb.com/catalogsearch/advanced/" data-
action="advanced-search">
        Advanced Search    </a>
</div>
                    </div>
                </div>
            <div class="actions">
                <button type="submit"
                        title="Search"
                        class="action search">
                    <span>Search</span>
                </button>
            </div>
        </form>
    </div>
</div>
```

```
    }</script></div>   <div class="block block-search"><div class="block block-title">
<strong>Search</strong></div><div class="block block-content"><form class="form minisearch"
id="search_mini_form" action="http://m2.novusweb.com/catalogsearch/result/" method="get"><div
class="field search"><label class="label" for="search" data-role="minisearch-label">
<span>Search</span></label> <div class="control"><input id="search" data-mage-
init='{"quickSearch":{ "formSelector":"#search_mini_form",
"url":"http://m2.novusweb.com/search/ajax/suggest/",
"destinationSelector":"#search_autocomplete"} }' type="text" name="q" value=""
placeholder="Search entire store here..." class="input-text" maxlength="128" role="combobox"
aria-haspopup="false" aria-autocomplete="both" autocomplete="off"/><div id="search_autocomplete"
class="search-autocomplete"></div> <div class="nested"><a class="action advanced"
href="http://m2.novusweb.com/catalogsearch/advanced/" data-action="advanced-search">Advanced
Search</a></div></div></div><div class="actions"><button type="submit" title="Search"
class="action search"><span>Search</span></button></div></form></div></div><ul class="compare
```

- **Combining and minifying JavaScript and CSS**: As with the HTML code of your pages, Magento can reduce the server load when delivering JavaScript and CSS files by merging them into fewer files and minifying the code.

Don't hesitate to challenge your developer and your hosting provider to improve your site's speed. There are tools to help you measure site speed, such as Pingdoms' Website Speed Test (`http://tools.pingdom.com/fpt/`). Use the results of these tools to compare the results of various settings and configurations.

Summary

Sometimes, it seems as though you'll never finish building a new online store. The truth is, you won't. As your online business grows, you bring on more staff, you add more features, and you add more products and customers. You'll always need to pay attention to the security and optimization of your store. More than anything, these are items that can truly make or break your success.

Throughout this book, you've been exposed to a great many tools, techniques, and terminology. By now, you've realized that e-commerce can be complicated. Fortunately, Magento 2, combined with the lessons of this book, can make the experience pay off!

The next and final chapter is a checklist to launch a new store. With your new knowledge of Magento, it's time to take the plunge!

10
Startup Checklist

You may be using this book as an ongoing reference to operate an existing Magento 2 store. We certainly hope that you have found it to be a comprehensive reference as well as a source of helpful advice.

On the other hand, you may be starting your own new Magento 2 store. Your developer has installed and performed the initial design and configuration tasks. You're now faced with completing the prelaunch activities that will enable customers to *shop*—and *buy*—on your store.

While going through this book chapter by chapter would get you to the point of operating a live, active online web store, it can be helpful to have a checklist to make sure you don't overlook any key aspects. In fact, a checklist is one of the most important things we give to our clients and a tool we use ourselves for our own stores. Even though we know e-commerce and Magento 2, we're not beyond using a checklist to ensure success.

This checklist will cover several key areas you need to manage:

- Product catalogs
- System configurations
- Products
- Content
- Communications
- Security

Obviously, there's a lot more you can do to leverage Magento's power; this checklist focuses on the *must-haves* required by a functioning website.

This list is also aimed at you, the store owner more than you, the developer. However, we encourage you to share this checklist with your developer as you may need their assistance with some items.

Setting up product catalogs

Before you begin, you need to establish the product catalogs you may need, especially if you're going to have more than one Website entity in your installation. Refer to `Chapter 3`, *Catalogs and Stores*, for guidance.

System configuration tasks

`Chapter 2`, *Settings and Configuration*, guides you through a myriad of system configuration panels in the Magento 2 backend. The following is a list of the key panels we feel you should address prior to launching.

Stores | All Stores

In `Chapter 3`, *Catalogs and Stores*, you learned how to create the various Website and Store entities and Store Views that you might need in your installation.

Stores | Configurations

 If you have more than one Website or Store View in your installation, be sure to pay attention to your Store View setting as you work on your configurations.

As you discovered in `Chapter 2`, *Settings and Configuration*, there are lots of panels within the Configuration section of the Magento 2 backend. Refer to `Chapter 2`, *Settings and Configuration*, for the configuration specifics, but before you launch, you should address each item on this list:

- **General** | **General**: Go here to update your specific store information
- **General** | **Web**: Go here to confirm these settings with your Magento developer

- **General** | **Currency Setup**: If you plan to use multiple currencies, be sure to set the currency conversion update process
- **General** | **Store Email Addresses**: Go here to update the e-mail addresses for the listed roles
- **General** | **Contacts**: Go here to enable your Contact Us form, if you wish, and specify to whom these inquiries should be sent
- **Catalog** | **Catalog**: Go here to update each of these settings to reflect how you wish to leverage the product management promotion features of Magento
- **Catalog** | **Inventory**: Go here to set your default inventory management configurations
- **Catalog** | **XML Sitemap**: Go here to configure your sitemap so that Google and other search engines can best process your site's content
- **Catalog** | **RSS Feeds**: Go here to enable or disable various RSS feeds as needed

 If you do not have a specific use for an RSS feed, it's best to keep it disabled. Competitors may use it to discover changes in your product pricing and availability.

- **Catalog** | **Email to a Friend**: Go here to enable or disable this functionality and configure your desired parameters
- **Customers** | **Newsletter**: If you are planning on sending newsletters, you should review these settings
- **Customers** | **Customer Configuration**: You may want to consult with your Magento developer on the appropriate settings that provide an appropriate level of access and security for your customers
- **Customers** | **Wish List**: Go here to enable if desired and configure the settings
- **Customers** | **Promotions**: Go here to configure the default settings to generate promotional coupon codes. These can be overridden when creating promotions
- **Customers** | **Persistent Shopping Cart**: If you wish for customers to return to your store within a certain period of time and find that their shopping cart has retained the previously added items, you should enable and configure this feature
- **Sales** | **Sales**: Go here to review these general settings to reflect your sales process and how you wish for various totals to be reflected on order screens and printouts
- **Sales** | **Tax**: Go here to configure how taxes should be included or excluded in orders

- **Sales | Checkout**: These settings pertain to the various aspects of the checkout process
- **Sales | Shipping Settings**: Go here to set the primary origin from which you will ship
- **Sales | Multishipping Settings**: If you want to allow customers to ship their order items to more than one destination, you can enable this feature
- **Sales | Shipping Methods**: Refer to `Chapter 4`, *Preparing to Sell*, and configure shipping based on how you wish to communicate shipping costs and availability to your customers
- **Sales | Google API**: If you intend to use Google Analytics and/or AdWords with your store, you can enter the necessary account information by going here
- **Sales | Payment Methods**: Using `Chapter 4`, *Preparing to Sell*, as a guide, choose and configure the payment methods that you will allow on your website

Stores | Currency Rates

If you chose more than one currency to allow in the **General | Currency Setup** panel, you should go to this panel and update to reflect the most current currency conversion rates. By enabling the **Webservicex** service, your rates will be periodically updated based on the current currency conversion rates.

Stores | Customer Groups

Review and add, if needed, the additional customer groups to your installation. Customer groups are discussed in `Chapter 4`, *Preparing to Sell*.

Stores | Tax Zones and Rates

Before you begin selling, you need to make sure your sales tax calculation rates are up to date. Refer to `Chapter 4`, *Preparing to Sell*, for in-depth discussion about tax rates and configurations.

Stores | Tax Rules

Using the Tax Zones and Rates settings you configured, you next need to set up the rules for what customer groups and product classes are taxed.

Stores | Terms and Conditions

If you enabled terms and conditions by navigating to **Sales** | **Checkout** | **Checkout Options**, you will want to add the text of the terms and conditions to which you will ask your customers to agree.

System | Cache Management

During the building and design of your Magento store, your developer most likely had caching disabled. It's common practice so that the changes are immediately viewable without having to flush the Magento cache.

Review your cache settings with your developer, and if you're launching your store, you will most likely want to enable caching to speed up page rendering for your customers.

System | Index Management

In `Chapter 9`, *Security and Administration*, we described how indexing helps to speed up your store. Confirm with your developer that indexing is properly enabled and configured for automatic reindexing.

Finalizing products

You may already have many, if not all, of your products added to your store at this point. However, before you launch, it's good practice to go through the product-related features of your store so that you leverage the full marketing power of Magento.

For more details on product management features, refer to `Chapter 5`, *Products*.

Products | Categories

If you already have products added, your categories will most likely be already configured as well. However, you should now take the time to add category descriptions and images that can help communication with your customers and search engines. Experiment with the configurations to give your categories the most beneficial layout features.

Products | Catalog

Likewise, for products, you should review the names, descriptions, images, attributes, and prices for your products. You certainly want to provide your shoppers with robust and accurate information.

Adding content

Content encompasses a broad swath within an e-commerce site, as discussed in Chapter 7, *Content and SEO*. It is never misspent time when invested on reviewing and enhancing the content and SEO components of your store.

Before you launch, you should confirm that you included the following:

- A privacy policy
- Site use terms and conditions
- Shipping and return policies
- Information or tools for requesting support
- Contact information
- Information about your company

If you do not have experience with SEO-optimized content, you may want to employ an e-commerce content specialist to assist you so that your content is most effective.

Editing communications

What you send out to customers is very important to your brand. In Chapter 8, *Promotion and Communications*, we went into detail on how to manage the various communication features of Magento 2.

Marketing | Email Templates

Perhaps the most important e-mails you will send are the ones that your customers receive when they place an order. Not only do these e-mails communicate the order status, but they also help fortify your brand and reputation.

Take time to carefully review and craft outgoing e-mails that reflect your best customer-relationship-building features.

Securing your store

Before you make your store publicly available to the world, you do have to recognize that there are bad people intent on accessing your store's backend without authorization. Using `Chapter 9`, *Security and Administration*, as a guide, you should work with your Magento developer to install security according to best practices.

System | User Roles

Start by creating the various roles needed to operate your store. Use the list in `Chapter 9`, *Security and Administration*, as a starting point.

System | All Users

With your roles established, you can begin adding your users.

 It deserves repeating: create user accounts for each person who will access your backend. Never share credentials among users.

Summary

While this chapter is the shortest in the book, it is probably one of the most important. Just as a pilot goes through a checklist before taking off or landing an airplane, our Magento 2 checklist will allow you to make sure you have at least reviewed all the important considerations prior to launch.

Once you launch, we're sure you'll know that the work doesn't end there. E-commerce is evolving every day, and you have to work every day to keep up. However, the good news is that your store is built on one of the most premier platforms in the world!

Index

Lightning Source UK Ltd.
Milton Keynes UK
UKHW03f2327120618
324127UK00007B/504/P